REBELLION WITH PURPOSE

A YOUNG ADULT'S GUIDE TO THE IMPROVEMENT OF SELF AND SOCIETY

Richard V. Sidy

PRESS

• 380 RAIN TREE ROAD • SEDONA, AZ • 86336

Rebellion with Purpose

©1993 Richard Sidy

All Rights Reserved: No part of this publication may be reproduced, stored in a retrieval system, or transmitted in any form, by any means, electronic, mechanical, photocopying, recording or otherwise, without the permission in writing from the copyright owner or representatives designated by the copyright owner.

ISBN: 0-9633744-1-9

Library of Congress Catalog Number 92-085157

Printed in the United States of America

Cover Design: *Fine Point Graphics*
                         Sedona, Arizona

Printed by: *DATA Reproductions Corporation*
                    Rochester Hills, Michigan

Published by: **SNS Press**
                    Foundations of Unity
                    380 Rain Tree Road
                    Sedona, Arizona 86336
                    FAX (602)284-9055
                    United States of America

*Dedicated to those who want
to create a better future.*

TABLE OF CONTENTS

	Preface	7
	Introduction	13
I.	Telling Your Story	19
II.	Everything Is Life	51
III.	Failing Is Not a Right	67
IV.	Freedom	75
V.	Living the Good Life	89
VI.	Finding the Path	101
VII.	Friendship, Love, Marriage, and Sex	121
VIII.	What Is The Role of Sacrifice in Our Life?	143
IX.	How to Prepare for the Future	165
	Glossary	179
	Suggested Reading	181
	Index	183
	About the Author	189
	Other Works by the Author	190

PREFACE

For the last twenty years, I have spent most of my days with teenagers. Actually, I have taught from pre-school children through adults in all types of situations and from all types of backgrounds, but mostly I have spent my days with teenagers. During this time, I have seen many triumphs and many defeats. I have seen tears of happiness and tears of pain. I have seen young people find themselves and I have seen them lose themselves.

We have weathered many storms together: classmates killed or paralyzed in gang shootings, drugs, pregnancies, dysfunctional families, abuse, suicides. Also, we have hugged each other with tears of joy in our eyes for the accomplishments nurtured by love, perseverance, and faith. There have been many discussions, many discoveries, many hard-headed battles, and much personal growth all-around.

People have asked me how I can take the stress and highly charged atmosphere of teaching teenagers. I always reply that compared to most types of work, teaching is a privilege because each day you are faced with the future. Young people have so many beautiful qualities, they are so curious and excited about life, they can be so outrageous, and they even have an innocence no matter how much hard life has crossed their path.

Even with the best plans you never know what to expect. Teenagers amplify the moods, the expectations, the problems, and the concerns of society. The classroom is the focal point for all that is going on in society. If there are storms and disasters, factories closed, war, civil unrest, land disputes, environmental problems, diseases, or economic ups and downs, they all walk through your door each hour of each day. There is a difference between the school day and the evening news, however. In the school the problems have faces. In those faces, no matter how harsh the reality, one can see hope.

Hope is the spiritual food for youth. Tomorrow will be better. No matter that adults are leaving them a legacy of debt, pollution, depletion of natural resources, decayed cities, and a new world disorder. Somehow in the heart of each young person is the anticipation that his or her future will be better than the present forecasts might indicate. Why? Are they crazy? Perhaps idealism and the desire for a better tomorrow make a person a little crazy. Yet, young people live for the future — that is where their dreams will become reality. Why else do they want to escape the garden of childhood for the asphalt, concrete, and synthetic carpet of adulthood?

The world looks different to a teacher than to most people. First of all, in order to survive, a teacher must have hope and some of the craziness and excitement of kids. Second, a teacher must see the big picture. He or she must see the future in every person and in all events. A teacher must be a bridge with feet in the present and arms reaching for the future.

The hopes and the demands of the kids themselves make us be a bridge. The demands of young people are the same demands found in any seed that is growing. They are the demands of the life energy to crack the seed, push out of the earth, and bloom in the sun. Facing these forces, a teacher has to believe in and work for progress. Every day the world is viewed through the idealism and the excitement of growth. It is viewed through the experimentation with life and with personal identity. This charges the atmosphere with a mixture of expectation and apprehension. The highs can be very high and the lows can be totally frustrating and sometimes tragic.

It is the challenge of teachers and students to work together in this atmosphere, to nurture that youthful energy so that it propels the individual toward a successful future.

Society used to help in this process, but it now often seems like an adversary. The challenges of youth to pursue its ideals and cultivate its potentials used to have the support and the reinforcement of society. Now, society refers to youth as a "problem." Youth becomes a "problem" only when society stagnates, begins to decay, and thus does not give a vision to youth. Without a vision, young people have no way to channel their energies constructively, meet their needs, nor fulfill their hopes for the future.

When young people contribute their youthful energy to meeting the challenges of the future, society may be regenerated. Without the incentive, perspective, and constructive energy of youth there can be no concern for the future. Only people who think about the future will have the courage and leadership to solve the problems of society.

Many adults have the expertise and desire to meet the gigantic social, economic, and environmental challenges we face. However, as in all eras, it is the youth that will be the "soldiers" on the front lines of the battles. In the battle to improve life they will discover the roots of their purpose and develop their own qualities of leadership.

The first battle is the battle to overcome the brainwashing of a materialistic view of the world. This view causes selfishness, hopelessness, and a meaningless existence. In spite of being incessantly bombarded by gloomy images of great crises and problems in the world, youth must rebel against escaping into the imaginary well-being of materialism.

Joy and hope come from developing and releasing the potentials of the human spirit.

Optimism comes from being active in serving nature and humanity. The purpose in life is discovered as you free your heart and mind, and use your energy to create a better life for yourself and for others.

People who work each day with young people realize the precious treasures that they have. We are angered that youth is seen either as a "problem" or as a "market." We are angered that they are valued only as potential producers and consumers, as spare parts in a faltering economy. We are angered that they have been used as a "market" for everything from sex and drugs to the most high-tech creations of industry. The basic necessities of life and the means to obtain them have become distorted by the obsessions and symbols representing the glamorous life style in advertising. Many link their self-image and goals in life to these symbols.

Over the years as crises have arisen, schools and teachers have had to be the shock absorbers. At such times the lesson plans fly out the window and we are compelled to discuss our most essential concerns. These are moments that are electrified by the energy of the students' honesty, insight, questions, fears, and indignation. At these times young people unbury their feelings and thoughts and expose their souls. At these times the student becomes the text and teacher, and life becomes the subject of study. Students love these times. They cause introspection and inspiration and open windows of thought and understanding. The BIG questions are put on the table, and the students become philosophers, lawyers, and surgeons.

This book was born from such discussions with young people over the years. It deals with many of the challenges, opportunities, and obstacles that young people are facing or will face in the future. It addresses many of the important questions about life. It emphasizes that life has purpose and that each individual also has a purpose to fulfill. It is in finding and expressing that purpose that one finds true friendship, happiness, and fulfillment in life. It encourages becoming an active part in improving society, to help restore optimism and commitment to improve society.

After reading the manuscript for this book, my adult friends and colleagues said that this book is not just for young adults. They pointed out that it is for anyone who is interested in developing his or her potentials and independence. It is for anyone who is concerned with a better future and who wants to be a part of creating it.

So may it be!

— **Richard V. Sidy**
Sedona, Arizona
Spring 1993

INTRODUCTION

When our children were young, we used to check out jig-saw puzzles from the public library. We had great fun fitting the pieces together, and it took great effort to stick with it until they were complete. Once they were done, we were so proud that we would not want to take them apart.

One time, after working many days on a particularly large and difficult puzzle, we were fitting the last pieces into their places with great anticipation and excitement, when we discovered that a couple of pieces were missing! We were so angry! How could a person ruin it for us by losing some pieces? It spoiled the whole puzzle for us to see a jagged hole where a part of the picture should have been. Those few missing pieces were more important than all the nine hundred and ninety-seven others, because *they* would have completed the picture.

I feel the same way about people as I did about those puzzle pieces. Each one has a purpose, each one is important. I see humanity and nature as a big picture. As a teacher, when I see a young person find his or her right place in the puzzle, I feel great joy. On the other hand, when a young person is lost, fails, commits crimes or suicide, or tries to fit into a false picture or into the wrong place, I feel a great sadness, even anger.

❖

*Imagine trying to put together
a puzzle with no idea of
the picture you are trying to make!*

❖

Why would anyone, knowingly or willingly, lose him or herself, or try to fit into the wrong place? Such behavior is the result of confusion and the distortion of reality. The growth of crime and abuse, corruption, pollution, and waste are symptoms of confusion psychologically, socially, and politically. Imagine trying to put together a puzzle with no idea of the picture you are trying to make! Unfortunately, most people and even nations are living a haphazard life with no clear concept of where it will go.

When a clear picture is lacking, we are at the mercy of those who we let make the pictures for us. The result is many competing and distorted pictures, created by people who have distorted or self-serving motives. Their false puzzle images have been forced upon humanity for greedy reasons. Life has been "packaged" so that we are forced into living in such a style as to recreate the image on the outside of the "package."

Now, people have to become distorted themselves to "fit" these false puzzles which they think are real. When people create false images of themselves to fit other people's reality or value system, they instinctively reject their behavior without really knowing why. The resulting inner conflict creates a lower self-image, depression, guilt, and confusion. These feelings then reinforce and justify apathy, negativity, failure, defensiveness, self-destructive behavior and even illness. We see these symptoms on a broad social scale today, affecting entire populations.

I know a young man whose parents are very athletic and active in sports. He neither is athletic, nor does he enjoy sports. His parents have forced him to participate in activities at which he has been unsuccessful. The result is that the boy feels that he is a failure. He has a terrible self-image, and now is failing academically. His handwriting is sloppy and reflects his low self-esteem and lack of pride. He is apathetic and has become chronically ill. This tragedy is the result of him trying to fit into the wrong place in the puzzle. It has distorted his image of himself and of his worth.

To have avoided this destruction of a young life, the parents should have been sensitive to the boy's true talents, abilities, and interests, and helped him develop those rather than impose their desires upon him. If he had experienced success and had developed his talents, he would be aware of where he fits in life; he would have a sense of direction and purpose rather than having been lost.

❖

*The essence of freedom and success is
to know oneself, and to know
where one fits in the big picture.*

❖

Everyone has a place and something valuable to contribute. Without each and every person doing his or her part, the picture is incomplete. People must resist false images which are imposed by selfish or vain people. Whole societies can lose their direction and purpose, and degenerate under the control of mis-guided, distorted, and egotistic "leaders."

On a grand scale, the media have been used to impose false or distorted values and images upon entire societies. These forces oppose the freedom and success of individuals and of whole cultures.

Throughout history up to the present day, societies have become obsessed by false images and false goals, imposed upon them by a powerful few or by their own overpowering desires. Obsession leads to wrong motives and wrong efforts. Wrong motives and wrong efforts lead to the wrong use of resources and talents. Socially, this wrong direction manifests through social degeneration, budget deficits, pollution, and the ultimate destruction of culture, and through increased hardships and suffering of people.

❖

*The goal of life is to see the big picture,
to know one's place in it,*

*and to cooperate to
make the picture complete.
The saying that
"a nation without vision perishes"
describes this truth,
and is also true for individuals.*

❖

One's vision is knowing one's value and place in the big picture, and developing the skills to be able to cooperate with the other jig-saw pieces in order to complete the picture. It is my hope that what follows will help the reader discover the big picture, find his or her place, and create a life of freedom and success for him or herself and for others.

CHAPTER I

TELLING YOUR STORY

Once a father was reading a story to his son about a lion, who was relentlessly pursued by hunters. In the end, the lion was killed. The little boy asked, "Why at the end of the story is the lion always killed? I thought that the lion was King of the jungle!" "Son," replied the father, "The lion will always get killed at the end of the story until he learns to tell his own story."

❖

The false self is built by false values that others impose upon us in order to control us.

❖

This story can be viewed as symbolic of the struggle of our real Self, or soul, to express itself against those who would capture it. Life tries to hunt down and kill our real Self or our soul. The real Self cannot be killed, but It may stay hidden as one builds up a false self. The false self is built by false values that others impose upon us in order to control us. We often willingly accept these values as our own because of our desire for acceptance. If others build our self-image, then they have in their power all the push-buttons needed to make us do what they want us to do.

The "lion" must learn to tell its story. Our lion is our nobility, our courage, our inner power, our virtues. Symbolically, lions have throughout history been used to represent great, royal houses. So our own inner lion must learn to express *itself*, to tell *its* story. How can this lion escape the deadly traps in life? How can it express itself and *tell* its story?

First, we must know what are the traps and second, learn to recognize the warnings as we live our life from day to day. The traps are set by certain vices of the personality, such as vanity and selfish desire. Some desires which do not seem bad can also lead us into traps: the desire to be accepted; to be loved; to be held in high esteem; the desire for pleasure; to be popular; to have fun. Such desires can give others the keys to control us. We know that advertising uses methods which appeal to these desires in order to get us to buy various products — whether they be candy, soda, hamburgers, cosmetics, clothes, cars, or whatever. They promise that our desires will be fulfilled by having what they sell. The motive of advertising is to get you to continuously use products by making them part of your image.

❖ TELLING YOUR STORY ❖ 21

We think that the purpose of advertising is to sell a product, but this is not so. Advertising sells a life style or a value system in which its product plays an important part. It creates a "big picture" in which its product is an essential puzzle piece. So, psychologically, a person adopts the life style or values advertised and thus needs the products which are props in the scene. Sadly, the person also becomes a prop used to tell the advertiser's story. He builds a false self, and, like the lion, has others "write his story."

Some people also impose history upon new generations just as advertisers impose their story. So much of history is the story of national, racial, and religious hatred; of wars and of intrigues; of examples of a powerful group using people for selfish or nationalistic interests. The result is that history has perpetuated feuds, fears, hatreds, jealousies, and undeserved pride. If young people "buy in" to this history by making it their own self-image, then they become the armies whose bodies will continue to bloody the pages of history and perpetuate historical traps.

❖

How can you not be a prop in the false, anti-survival life style of advertising and history?

❖

Learning to tell your story helps you avoid these pitfalls. This means to live a life which you create in fulfilling your true purpose. An adopted self-image should not shape your values or life style, but your true values should result in your image and life style.

All people need heroes and role models. This is why it is so important to find role models whose lives really represent values which bring out your highest potentials and goals. Most of the "role models" for young people are packaged desires in human forms. They represent fantasy rather than reality. People imitate their appearance, mannerisms, likes and dislikes, and create their "image." At some point in one's life it is necessary to stop this dress-up play, this conformity. Often people choose role models just so that they be accepted by others.

❖

Role models are not for imitating.

❖

A role model ought to serve as an example of characteristics and values which lead to success and to the opportunities and choices which reveal your own hidden abilities and inner powers. Your power is your unique potential to fulfill a unique place in life. Role models can bring out your character by *who* they are, not by *what* they are. Be inspired by their example if it is worthy but don't try to be their clone.

You "tell your story" through living your life. Your life is your story. If your life is imitation, then your life is *his*-story, not *your* story. If your life is the result of being manipulated by false images imposed upon you by others and aimed at stimulating your desires, then your life is just a prop in a marketing campaign. However, if you find your purpose and understand the character traits and values which lead you to your purpose, you will really be able to tell your story through your life. You will not become the lion killed by hunters at the end of the story.

❖

You create your life through your power to think and through the understanding of your heart.

❖

In order to write your story, your mind must be free to accurately know the world and your place in it. You create your life through your power to think and through the understanding of your heart. These parts of your nature help you shape your goals and actions. Many people in society are satisfied with acquiring the possessions which symbolize their desired image but lack the abilities or actions which merit those possessions. They are like the fleas sitting on the king's horse who thought that all the people were bowing to them as the king rode through the village.

❖

One's true merit is a natural result of one's goals, skills, and actions.

❖

A person with goals but no skills cannot achieve the goals or unlock the potentials in his or her life. Clear thinking is necessary in order to have honest, realistic goals, and to see what skills are needed to reach them. An understanding heart gives a person a sense of proportion, creates a positive attitude toward life, and develops a sense of responsibility. A clear mind and an understanding heart can be developed and work together to help a person take control of his or her life.

Sometimes people have the attitude that they are just the products of chance: that they are lucky or unlucky; that they were born into rich families or poor families; that they have good parents or bad parents; that they are smart or dumb. They have a feeling that life is a card game, and that fate has dealt them their hand. They feel that whatever life they have is out of their control. Such people have a difficult time really tapping in to their inner power and purpose.

❖

How can one change the idea of fate into the idea that one can create his or her own "luck?"

❖

How is it possible that one can create his or her own "luck?" First, it is important to reject the idea that you are the product of chance. Nothing so complex as a unique human being with a unique personality, a unique set of talents, and a unique set of life challenges can happen by accident. This idea limits your possibilities and self-concept and also takes responsibility out of your hands. Second, you need to understand that whatever your circumstances, good or bad, you have to improve and prove your own merit.

Let's say that you were born with intelligence, talents, and material comfort. This is a great bank account, but how will you spend it? I once had a student who was classified as "gifted" but was barely passing my class. After receiving his progress report, he very indignantly came to me and demanded, "Why did you give me this grade? Don't you know that I'm gifted?" I answered, "You're gifted? So give me some gifts!" "You don't understand," he whined, "I'm *gifted*!" "OK," I said, "You're *gifted*. Where are your gifts? If one is gifted, one must have gifts to give."

I also have taught kids who were classified as educationally handicapped, who took difficult classes against the advice of counselors and parents — and succeeded through sheer guts. In both cases, others were trying to write their stories by classifying them.

The idea that one can create one's own "luck," in spite of the cards one was dealt in life, is an idea that can make you free. It can free you from the limits of classifying yourself or of letting yourself be classified. It can also make you a more active person by challenging you to tell your own story: to take life as a challenge, as an exciting adventure.

Many people become bored in life and, no matter what escapes they try, they are never satisfied. They go shopping, they go to the movies, to ball games, to restaurants, to parties. The problem is that at the end of each activity, they are right back where they started: bored. All their time, energy, and money are spent on being a prop in a scene. In order to not be bored, you have to make yourself interesting — create interests and goals.

❖

You can't conquer boredom by being a spectator in life or by being a part of the scenery.

❖

You can think of the way many people live as playing a video game. It is so funny to observe people playing electronic games. They think they are playing the game, but in fact the game is playing them. The game causes them to push certain buttons, to get certain rewards. The game makes them aggressive, happy, frustrated, and emotional. It makes them excited and creates all the behavior needed for the game. The person becomes almost hypnotized, and in the extreme cases people become almost insane, addicted, obsessed by the game. The player loses his identity in being played by the game, in being a slave of the game. The game is totally unreal, yet it becomes so real for the player that it becomes something to live for, a major goal in life. At the end of the game, the button pusher either won or lost but remains the same bored and boring person.

People who live life like such a game never make progress or tap their inner resources. They are actually the game pieces played by the big players: the politicians, the manufacturers, the business speculators, the organized criminals. This is not freedom. This is just "playing the game."

❖

The goals are destinations, but the most important thing is what happens to you on your journey to your goal.

❖

In order to write your story, you have to create interests and goals, then work to achieve them. The goals are destinations, but the most important thing is what happens to you on your journey to your goal. When you reach a goal, you will realize that the goal is not so great, but that you are greater for having made the journey.

This is like growing up. A seven year old has the goal of being a teenager. A teenager seems so big, so free, so exciting. When the child does become a teenager, he or she realizes that it's no big thing; that there are new, more important goals. The teenager thinks about being an adult. However, when the child becomes the teenager, the child is a different person.

The journey from childhood to adolescence is a time of growth, of new abilities and responsibilities, of new interests, and new understandings. Not only has the child's body changed and grown, but the child's world has grown. The borders of the known world have expanded as well as the child's awareness of his or her place in that world. It is this process of growth and change that is most significant in human development and in a person's developing sense of self and attitude in life.

Adolescence is an important time in one's life to stop, to take an account of where you have been and where you are going. Many have characterized adolescence as a restless time, a rebellious time, a searching time; a time of experimentation; a time of having dreams for the future; a time of hope and a time of crisis. It is a time of forming your adult personality, and of making choices that will shape your future. It is a time of developing standards that will lead you to success or failure in education, in work, in marriage, and in your community. It is a time of adopting your own set of values and outlook on life, of developing tastes and interests that will be shaped into life goals.

It is really important, then, to find out who you are, how you got to be that way, what you want to be, what you need to change, and what you need to keep the same.

❖

When you take time to check yourself out, you will be making a very important step in taking charge of your life, in becoming the author of your story.

❖

Most of our days are spent cruising on automatic pilot, acting and reacting according to our pre-programmed push-buttons. Occasionally it is important to check if our programming is really taking us where we want to go. It is good to make changes in our lives that will bring us closer to our purpose. Sometimes we have experiences that help us develop a new point of view on our life.

A young man I know changed because of a trip to a foreign country. Before he left, he was "in love" with his girlfriend. His love was a mixture of friendship, shared interests, shared values, happiness that someone was interested in him, and pity for the problems that she had. The problem was that their relationship was mainly a way to reinforce their habits. They dressed the same, liked the same things, had the same attitudes. Their emotional needs for each other — his, to be accepted and liked; hers, to have someone to depend on — made them feel good about themselves and about each other.

When he took the trip, he saw his relationship in a new light from a distance. In a new environment, he could not lean on the crutches of his habits. He had to respond to people differently and he had to depend on himself more. He found that he could not live life on automatic because his previous programming didn't fit his new circumstances. His push-buttons didn't work. There were new expectations, new needs, and new experiences. He found that people were really interested in him and that he had much to offer. He made new friends. He then realized that his love for his girlfriend was not only a comfortable habit, but it was a case of dependency on both of their parts. This dependent relationship prevented them from growing and from discovering their own power — from being able to depend on themselves. The result of this experience was that he realized that he did not really "love" the girl, but that they could be friends.

❖

Taking the time to check ourselves out will help us to tell our story with more accuracy and interest.

❖

We can't all go on a trip to a foreign country in order to discover ourselves. Yet we can create the same distance in our minds by traveling to new lands within ourself. We can create this mental attitude when we take the time to check ourself out, see where we have come from, check our programming, and think about our destination. Taking time to do this will help us build the foundation for our future, will help us tell our story with more accuracy and interest.

When we want to take control of our life, make our own luck, we may check out our programming using the following checklist.

1. What are the desires which are controlling me?

2. Who or what are my role models?
3. What symbols am I using to classify myself or to cause others to classify me?
4. What is my general attitude toward life?
5. Am I holding on to negative or bitter feelings about those who have hurt me in the past?
6. Do I recognize those who have helped me?
7. What do I have, to give to others?

By going through this checklist, we can get a better picture of our false self, our programming and our habits, and begin to express our true Self, our goals, and our purpose. We need to free ourselves from the traps that the hunters of our spirit have set for us, so that our soul-lion can let roar its noble voice.

1. What are the desires which are controlling me?

When we identify the desires which are controlling us, we can begin to control them. Desires are of three types: physical, emotional, and mental.

Physical desires are the desires to have more and more: more food, more clothing, more possessions, more excitement. The things that we desire are natural drives and are things we need to survive physically.

These are not bad when you control them and they assist you in reaching your goals.

Problems with necessities occur when they become the goal of life, when they become automatic habits, or when they become preoccupations. Sometimes we use our physical necessities to satisfy our emotional needs so that they take on a glamorous and symbolic dimension.

An example would be the need for shoes. Although a basic need, some people will spend hundreds of dollars for big name shoes which give them status and prestige. When we meet a basic need in an extravagant way just to satisfy our emotional need to be accepted or admired, the need starts to control us and shape our behavior. This is how obsessions or uncontrolled drives are created.

If you feel that your physical needs and desires are controlling your life, ask yourself: "What physical desires do I have? Are they helping me reach my goals in life? Are they causing me to fail or to create harmful relationships? Are they necessary? Can I live and be happy without satisfying them? Are they forcing me to do things I prefer not to do? Are they causing me to waste my time, money, or health? Are my desires habits, or are they coming from pressures outside of myself? Is the way in which I satisfy my physical needs and desires turning into my self-image?"

❖

When physical and emotional forces

join together to build our "image," our behavior comes under the control of an obsession.

❖

Emotional desires are built around the need to be loved and to love. *When people become possessive and greedy in satisfying their emotional needs, they get out of control and their emotions blow them here and there like a violent tempest.* Emotional moods control relationships, and life is lived as a volleyball between the opposing teams of happiness and sadness, between love and hate, between friendship and jealousy.

Uncontrolled emotions result in selfishness and insecurity. When we are selfish emotionally, we become insincere and uncaring of others' feelings. Because of our own selfish and insincere feelings, we become distrustful of others' feelings toward us. This results in relationships in which we feel doubtful, jealous, or touchy. Our lack of ability to build emotional bonds with others whom we can trust makes us unhappy, dissatisfied, lonely, cold, and unloved.

When we are driven to satisfy our emotional desires by accumulating physical possessions, it is a sign that our relationships with people are unsuccessful. We want to feel happy and we want others to think that we are happy. Our physical possessions then become symbolic of the happiness we desire or symbolic of the love we wish we had. Emotional desires create emptiness and actually kill one's ability to be sensitive to others, to give love, and to be happy. We try to cover this emptiness up by having more and more glamorous possessions.

❖

The secret and mystery of satisfaction is that one is only satisfied by giving.

❖

When a person is possessive, he or she will try to gain satisfaction but never achieve it. When we think about meeting the needs of others rather than about our own comfort, recognition, and happiness, we will gain the keys to our own emotional fulfillment. Giving opens the gates of joy because it opens the heart. The heart is the source of life energy and of love. It is the heart that unites us with others. Emotions resulting from self-centeredness such as jealousy, greed, anger, fear, hatred, and self-pity isolate us and close our heart. We can conquer these monsters by loving, selfless actions toward others.

Uncontrolled *mental desires* for power and recognition lead to selfish competition and to the manipulation and exploitation of others. A selfish ego uses the mind as its slave to achieve its goal of superiority. Mental desire puts the individual at the center of the universe. All activities then become self-serving. The mental desires dominate the body and emotions and use them to satisfy one's own ego. Similarly, the knowledge of the mind tries to dominate other people and use them to satisfy the ego's desire for pleasure, power, and recognition. When ego dominates the personality, you lose your sense of value, judgment, and spiritual direction.

❖

When we are under the influence of our spiritual nature, our body, emotions, and mind are used to benefit others.

❖

As was stated, the desires of the body, emotions, and mind are natural and necessary for survival. The problem and danger to our spiritual nature is when they are not under our control, or are under the control of others who want to use us. When the need to satisfy our physical, emotional, or mental desires becomes the major goal in our life, we become the slave to those desires and lose our purpose. This will be discussed in more depth in the chapter on freedom.

It is important for us to identify those influences which are controlling us so that we can see if they are helping us to reach our goals or are preventing us from reaching them.

2. **Who or what are my role models?**

I had a student once who was very negative about life and quite depressed. She was an attractive girl and very intelligent. Yet she was making herself ugly by the way she dressed and how she used cosmetics. She was a real riddle for me. She was so argumentative and defensive for no reason and would not respond to kindness.

When she turned in her notebook, I saw that it was covered with pictures of her favorite rock group and with phrases that were very negative and destructive. The members in the rock group were really ugly — monsters. And their ugly faces were grimacing in the most repulsive way as they sang. Their faces were at once sad, full of hate, and devouring. On the pages of her work were sketches she had made — all images of death and distorted forms.

Once she brought in a cover from one of their record albums to show her friends because it had the words to the songs printed on the back as well as some group photos. Looking at their faces, I saw no kind look, no joy, no happiness, no beauty. Just dark and ugly emotions and dirty sex. The words of the songs were full of hate and sexual attacks. No love, no compassion, no respect, no appreciation, no vision of a better future.

I found out that this girl had their pictures all over her locker and from floor to ceiling in her room, and that she listened to their destructive songs day and night. She even had a huge poster of them on the ceiling above her bed so that she would fall asleep each night with their image in her eyes.

This girl is back on track now but after taking herself and family through the hell of hopelessness, conflict, attempts at suicide, and insanity.

This is an extreme, but not a rare example of how role models or idols can control a life. They can shape a person's values or self-image for better or for worse depending on what they stand for. Through many ages of human history, the idols or role models of societies shaped cultures and led to either a birth of culture and prosperity or to destruction for whole nations or empires.

Whether role models be positive or negative, they may exert control over us. This is not just because we imitate them, but because they present an image and value system which deeply impress us psychologically and condition our choices, attitudes, behavior, health, and even how we look. Real, positive role models do not make us imitate, but they help us bring out the qualities we admire from within ourselves.

❖

*It is important to check out
the signs in our life which show us
who our role models are and
how much they are helping or preventing
us from reaching our goal.*

❖

The signs are those things and values around which we are building our image: how we dress, what we are working for, what we spend our money on, how we relate to others, and our attitude toward life.

We must always keep in mind that even positive role models are only examples, and that we must work to be equal to them or to surpass them. Our destiny, our place in the puzzle of life is unique. Even a role model had a role model or a goal he or she was working to achieve. We cannot pay due respect to our positive role models simply by imitating them. We have to make their image and value in our life *real* through our own efforts and through fulfilling our own higher purpose in life.

3. **What symbols am I using to classify myself or to cause others to classify me?**
Symbols can be the way we dress, how we talk, the things that we have, and even our behavior and the way we work. Symbols are the outer signs of our likes and dislikes, of our goals, of our self-image, of where we would like to fit in life.

We use symbols to communicate in a definite way something indefinite and mysterious: who we are. If we really are ourselves, our symbols should present a fairly accurate picture of our inner nature, our abilities, and our goals.

❖

Sometimes we adopt symbols to use because we want to be accepted and to belong to groups who have those symbols.

❖

It must be remembered that the more definite the symbols we use, the more people will define and classify us. They will think they know us without even making the effort to do so.

The symbols that we use to communicate ourselves are limiting. They limit us in the minds of others, limit their expectations, and limit how they relate to us. Eventually they condition how we relate to ourselves and to others, too. Symbols contribute to stereotyping and prejudice.

❖

If people totally identify with the symbols they use to communicate their image, then they will really limit the options and opportunities they meet in life.

❖

We see that in high school society students conform to certain group symbols, become classified, and are not really free to move from one group to another. Cliques form around symbols, and the members of cliques often have difficulty in changing their image or in having people really get to know them. We just simply classify people and put them in their pigeon hole and think we know them. We say, "Oh, so and so? Yeah I know him, he's a . . . (jock, surfer, gangbanger, preppy, hippy, cowboy, mod, nerd, black dude, chicano, or so forth). . . . "

I knew this guy at my high school during the early days of surfing, when to be a surfer you really had to be part of a sub-culture — dress and act in a certain way. Well, he surfed but nobody knew because he never talked about it, and he dressed in a generic way. He studied hard and took difficult classes and hung around with kids in his class. One day he was with some surfers and mentioned that he surfed. They all said, "You? Surf? What kind of a kook are you anyway? You don't look like a surfer." They started making fun of him and putting him down.

    He challenged them, "How can you make fun of my surfing if you've never seen me surf? Why don't we all meet at County Line next Saturday and have a little contest!" Well, none of the surfers knew that this generic, studious guy had been surfing for four years almost every day in the summer and frequently throughout the winter. The day of the contest came and the waves were steep and overhead. This generic guy had a hot day and out-surfed all the "surfers" who were putting him down. After that, nobody bothered him at school, and he had a reputation as a hot surfer even though he didn't play the part.

    This generic guy wouldn't let himself be classified. He could relate to different groups of kids on the basis of shared interests and not on the basis only of shared symbols. Because of his nondescript individuality, he forced people to really get to know him and what he was interested in and what he could do. He related with others on a more honest basis and was freer than others who communicated mainly through their symbols.

4. **What is my general attitude toward life?**
    Our attitude toward life may come from many sources: from our nation, race, religion, family, from our environment, from our personal economic situation, from our teachers, from the people we associate with, from the news, from advertising, from our role models, from our personal experiences, from our needs and desires.

    With so many possible sources from which we may form our attitude toward life, there is much room for confusion since many of the influences contradict each other.

    Attitude toward life is a major determiner of a person's motivation, of one's value system, of how one relates to others, of one's emotional and mental orientation, and of the life choices one makes. A person who grows up abused, in poverty, or in an insecure family situation will have a different outlook on life than a person who grows up in a secure and loving environment. A person whose nation is prosperous, wealthy, and stable will have a different attitude than one who grows up surrounded by war, poverty, and illness. A person who grows up in a city will have a different concept of life than one who grows up in a rural environment.

    Our parents, friends, national politics, religious orientation, and advertisers are all trying to tell us how to achieve the "good life" and motivate us to live by *their* values. Some use fear, some use the promise of reward, some appeal to our common sense, some appeal to our ego and desires, some appeal to our insecurities, some to our reason. How can we find our direction through this jungle?

❖

We must develop values that will lead us to achieving our purpose in life and to fulfilling our responsibilities to others.

❖

We need to see clearly the attitudes which influence us and see on what their motives are based. Attitudes are usually based upon optimism or pessimism, upon spiritual goals or upon materialistic ones, upon the desire to unify or to separate people, upon the desire to serve others or to use others, on the concept of an orderly universe or on the concept of chaos, on the desire for challenging oneself or on the desire for ease, on the desire to explore and be open to other people, environments, and ways of life or on the desire to believe that one's own way of life is the best and only way to live.

If we can for a moment stand free from all influences from the outside and free from all the selfish desires of our body, emotions, and mind, and stand free as a pure soul without nationality, race, or religion, we may better listen to our heart or inner voice that will guide us to the right attitude of life. That moment of pure freedom is like a light in the dark jungle of confusion and screeching monsters. It is like a birth out of the darkness of uncertainty and sleep into the light of wisdom.

❖

We can only make choices for the benefit of ourselves and others if we have a vision of the future.

❖

Many people, institutions, or forces try to shape our life attitude based on the past. Most want to limit us, mold us, and control us for their own purposes. When we achieve a moment of freedom, when we stand as a soul before the menu of life presented by others, we will be able to choose those values and attitudes which will enable us to unfold our inner beauty and the inner beauty of others whom we meet in life, and help build the future of our dreams.

5. Am I holding on to negative or bitter feelings about those who have hurt me in the past?

One cannot take a step forward on the path toward one's purpose unless one forgives those by whom one has been hurt. Bitterness, resentment, and hatred are like hooks in one's heart, holding one to past unpleasant memories thus controlling one's life.

❖

*Forgiveness gives permission to oneself
and to the one forgiven
to move forward without
guilt, fear, or hatred.
It cleans the path to one's goals and
cuts the chains with which one is
anchored to past failures.*

❖

Forgiveness requires love and compassion. These qualities are the fuel of life, propelling us toward our goals. Love and compassion help us work for the best interests of ourself and others. When we have negative attachments to the past by feelings of hurt, self-pity, or hatred, our "car" is filled with crazy hitchhikers who force us to drive in the opposite direction until we crash or reach a dead end.

Forgiveness frees us and others and is the foundation of peace. Peace is the condition of being able to use all of our resources for good works. If we don't have peace, we use our resources to destroy our enemies or to protect ourselves from them. We are then depriving ourselves of the benefits of all our potentials and of the potential resources from others who could be our friends and partners. Our life stagnates, becoming controlled by negative emotions. *Forgiveness unifies, resentment divides. In unity there is more power, freedom, and courage. These are moral resources needed for progress.*

Individuals and nations need to practice forgiveness in order to be able to write their stories. Without forgiveness, personal, national, and international history remains stuck in the same groove, repeating itself over and over and over like a broken record.

6. Do I recognize those who have helped me?

It is so important to see that every day there are many people, known or unknown, who help you. We come to expect everything to work. We expect the light to go on when we push the switch. We expect the supermarket shelves to be well stocked with food. We expect that if we have an accident, emergency personnel will come to our aid. We expect our schools, offices, and cities to be clean every day. Most of the time we don't even realize that things work because people are working to help others.

Natural forces are also our helpers whether they be visible or invisible. The sun, the rain, the oceans, the minerals, the plants and animals, the air we breathe, the cycles of the universe, and the movements of atoms work together to sustain life. If we eat a delicious meal, we should not only thank the cook but also the many elements which made the food to grow.

❖

Recognizing those who help is a powerful way to transform our life.

❖

Appreciation makes us see that we are not isolated beings. It makes us realize that we are parts of a vast, interconnected network of all created things. It makes us see that we are a piece of a great puzzle of life. This recognition creates three natural responses which bring one closer to an understanding of what life is about. These responses are

- the sense of gratitude
- the sense of respect
- the sense of responsibility

❖

Gratitude helps us see where we are in the big picture and helps us see how we are connected to other people and things.

❖

The sense of gratitude increases our love for others and our feeling of unity with them. When love and appreciation increase, we feel happier and more fulfilled. When we are grateful to the natural resources that sustain us, we become less wasteful and more protective of them. On the other hand, when we are not grateful we become wasteful and eventually will lose that for which we had no gratitude.

❖

Human dignity is not measured by what job one does, but in how one does it, and in how one's work contributes to the welfare of the whole.

❖

The sense of respect increases the dignity of others and also one's own dignity. Many so-called "lowly" jobs in society are absolutely necessary for the welfare of society. If, for example, janitors and rubbish collectors stopped working, then life would be miserable. If we respect the work of every part, then we develop appreciation for others.

Each job in an organization, society, or nation may help it reach its goals *if* it is in line with the purpose of that organization. According to this criterion, dignity and respect should be merited by the effect of one's work upon society. An engineer or company executive, who generally receive society's respect, do not deserve that respect if they create products that go against the benefit of society or that pollute the environment, causing pain and suffering to people and to nature. Movie stars who cause people to have "values" which do not help them fulfill their purpose should not be given more respect than the person who collects your trash each week. The sense of respect helps us put our values in order. We must not confuse wealth, fame, and status with the values which merit dignity and respect.

❖

Society should measure maturity not in terms of age but in the degree of responsibility a person shows.

❖

The sense of responsibility develops in us when we recognize how much we are helped by others. We see that we depend on others and that others depend on us. As children we are more taking than giving, but as we mature we begin to think about what role we will play as adults. In fact, the sense of responsibility is a great sign of maturity.

Responsibility is a result of seeing that in order to be happy, successful, and respected in life we have to find where we fit so that we fulfill our role in helping others reach their purpose.

❖

We achieve happiness, success, and respect by making others achieve happiness, success, and respect.
This should be the foundation of anything we do.

❖

7. What do I have, to give to others?

Everyone has much to give others. The greatest gifts are love, gratitude, hope, joy, and encouragement. This is the fuel others need to move ahead. These gifts are the buried treasures of our soul. When we give them to others, we increase them in ourselves. *This is the magic of doing good. We multiply the good in ourselves by giving it away!*

It is also important to see the needs of others and do things to meet their needs. Sometimes this takes no special skill, and sometimes you will have to train many years to gain the skills which you need to help others.

❖

*Whatever you choose as a career,
you will be more fulfilled and happy in it
if you have the attitude that
you are meeting the needs of others.*

❖

All work that is necessary can be done in such a way as to give joy and happiness to others. The man who cleans my room at school does so with such energy and dedication! He does a thorough job, always does extra, and works with great happiness. All the teachers in our hall treat him with gratitude and respect because he takes his job very seriously. His work enables us to do our job better and gives teachers and students a healthier and more beautiful school environment. His work is an important piece in the big picture of educating young people.

❖

*When we give to others by our own
free will, we are writing our own story.*

❖

Giving is an expression of our soul qualities. Giving also builds our character and brings out our potential power to be in control of our life. Giving opens many doors and makes a person independent. Think about it! When you are only taking, you become dependent upon those who are giving to you. You can be controlled by them and *they* write your story by what they give. When we do jobs just to earn money or other rewards, we can be used to even do things we hate or to do things that harm society and nature. *If you see people who are unhappy in their work, you will see it is because they are not there to give but only to take.* Whatever you do, you can be fulfilled if you work with skill, care, and an attitude of meeting the needs of the people you work with and of the people you serve.

❖

*Telling your story is an act of expressing your true Self.
It is an act of freedom.*

❖

Freedom is the fulfillment of one's purpose in life. The great human tragedy throughout history has been that most people are born, live, and die controlled by others. People have been used. People have had their story written by others. The noble lion of the human spirit has been caged by hunters for sport and personal wealth. The human spirit craves to be free. It craves identity, and it craves to be of service to nature and to humanity. In order to really exist, one has to satisfy the craving of one's spirit. This comes through discovering your true and noble Self.

CHAPTER II

EVERYTHING IS LIFE

Young people ask the most challenging questions! Many of them are the same ones with which philosophers and scientists have been occupied for ages. One of the most frequent questions asked is if life exists in other places in the universe.

❖

What we know about life and the universe is constantly growing and changing.

❖

As our horizons expand, our spiritual insights continue to grow and expand as well. The definition of life is growing as people explore and reveal new dimensions of awareness. Religious faith as an expression of an unseen dimension of life is becoming more personal and more factual everyday. It is going beyond the doctrines and worship of established religions. Science, too, is breaking down the barriers of the material world and exploring unseen foundations of the universe.

The concept of life is becoming less and less limited by the old material concept of nature. This materialistic view was created by man's limited senses and inability to deal with worlds beyond his immediate day-to-day experience. There was simply life and there was death. Life was to exist and death was the end of life. Moreover, man categorized life into three levels: plant life, animal life, and human life. "Life" was then defined according to the common biological function these three categories shared: respiration, eating, digesting, and reproducing.

*The invisible energies are
creative forces
which are responsible for
form, for health, and for
the laws of behavior of both
thinking and non-thinking beings.*

In the twentieth century, thinkers and explorers in the fields of psychology, religion, philosophy, and the sciences have discovered new foundations of life, and have expanded man's awareness so that these could be understood. These explorers use different names for this foundation of life but they are all talking about the same thing. Psychologists call it psyche or psychic energy. Religious people call it Spirit or God. Philosophers call it the first principle, cause, or consciousness. Scientists call it energy. Whatever it is called, it means that the visible world is like clothing for the invisible world. The invisible energies are creative forces which are responsible for form, for health, and for the laws of behavior of both thinking and non-thinking beings. Even things which we considered non-living are forms of spirit or energy.

❖

Everything is expressing life energy,
only in different forms,
in different colors,
with different degrees of complexity,
movement,
sensitivity,
and purpose.

❖

If we look at the universe in this way, then everything is alive. Even space is not empty. With the proper instruments we could detect that space is filled with electrical currents carrying all sorts of information, light, color, sound, thought, and emotions. We will also see that all these different forms and expressions of energy are following laws, have a purpose, and are important puzzle pieces in the big picture.

How can viewing the universe in this way answer our question, "Is there life anywhere else than on earth?" Well, it tells us that the universe is a great living system in which man is one form. This is like saying that the universe is a great symphony in which man is a note, a melody, or a refrain.

When we think about life, we can think about it as a life energy with many qualities of expression for many purposes. We can feel more connected with the universe, like we are little fish swimming in a great ocean of life. It gives us greater respect and appreciation for life; it gives a greater sense of relationship and interdependence; it gives a greater sense of responsibility to other forms of life. This eliminates a feeling of isolation and makes one feel more like a relative to all other beings and to the natural world.

We see in some cultures that have lived close to nature an understanding that the universe is one family in one spirit. The Sioux Indians have a beautiful expression, "With all things and with all beings we are as relatives." While living in a rural village in Africa, I discovered that the people had no separate word in their language for "fruit." Instead they called it "tree-child." Their custom before picking a fruit was to ask permission from the tree and then to thank the tree after they picked it. This shows a great respect for life and an awareness that man should not abuse other forms of life.

The golden rule which is in every religion shows also this awareness of oneness. "Do not unto others that which you would not have done unto you." This shows that all beings are one being. If you harm another you are harming yourself. In Christian traditions are the words Christ spoke. "I am in you, you are in me, we are in the Father one." Native Americans call the Father "the Great Spirit."

Others call that Spirit a Mother. In an ancient text of the *Upanishads* is the prayer that refers to this oneness as "... Thou, Who givest sustenance to the universe, from Whom all things proceed, to Whom all things return...."

Life on our planet is made possible by the Sun. Think how many stars are in the universe! Each star is a station relaying and transmitting all kinds of energy waves, filling the universe with life energy.

❖

*All wisdom and knowledge
come down to the following goals:
to understand life;
to know one's purpose
in relationship to the whole;
to know how to live a healthy,
secure,
and ethical life;
and to know how to relate to and express
the spirit in ourselves and in others.*

❖

One of the qualities of life is love. Love is a way of proving to yourself that everything is life. If you are really sincere and unselfish in love and love all beings and nature, then you will experience more the life energy. When you put love in action, you begin to serve others and nature. Death is isolation and self-centeredness. These are the causes of most depression and illness.

> *When you cut yourself off from
> the love of others
> and from nature,
> you lose energy.
> Giving
> and serving
> put you in the stream of love
> circulating in our planet.*

Love unifies, brings people together. Hate and jealousy separate and divide people. Even in atoms we see love expressed as magnetism which brings atoms together to form molecules, brings molecules together to form cells, and gradually builds greater and greater compounds and organisms. We see that there is great cooperation in the universe.

What are some practical steps a person can take to improve his or her own life after realizing that everything is life? How can the quality of love be put into action? There are several things a person can do to express love:

1. Work for unity
2. Work to increase cooperation
3. Work to protect people and nature
4. Work to improve the lives of others
5. Work for beauty

*When we realize that
everything is life
and that the same spirit lives in all beings,
we get a feeling of
more responsibility in our life.*

1. **Work for unity**

Unity goes from the individual level to the whole of humanity.

First, we must unify ourself. If we love ourself, we will take care of our health, we will not do things we know go against our conscience, and we will plan and organize our life in order to reach our goals. We will develop dependability, honesty, and trustworthiness.

Second, we will work for unity within the circle of our family and friends. This does not mean that we all become clones of each other. Unity is tolerance, respect, and appreciation for each person's individuality. Love in the family and amongst friends is concerned with each person's welfare and with the need to accomplish his or her goals.

Third, we will work for unity in our school and community. People can be brought together to meet common needs, to beautify their environment, and to work together on projects for the common good of the community. They can eliminate attitudes which divide people. Healthy disagreement is important in a community if people are willing to put the best interests of the community ahead of their personal opinions and work for consensus. An atmosphere of fairness, respect, and appreciation must prevail.

The principles of creating unity within ourself, within our family, and within our community need to be extended to our nation and to humanity in order to make love the prevailing motive in relationships.

❖

Human suffering is the result of the absence of love in relationships and in political policies.

The absence of love is the result of people feeling separate from others. Thus, unity is a primary necessity for creating the right conditions for life to flourish.

❖

2. **Work to increase cooperation**

If you've ever been part of a team you have an idea what cooperation is. You want each member to do his or her best and to be successful. You work together, you depend on each other, you encourage each other, and you help each other. On a team you realize that if a teammate is unhappy, having a bad day, or is hurting, the whole team suffers. On the other hand, a teammate who is having a great day picks everyone up. On a team you realize that each individual is important for the success of the whole.

Imagine if whole communities or nations felt that they were part of a team. Everyone would work together and help each other and take care of each other. Each person would be motivated to do his or her best for the team, and everyone would encourage each other. This team concept could eliminate racism, unemployment, poverty, and exploitation. It is based upon the concept of unity and responsibility, of working for a common goal.

What if nations and all of humanity felt they were on the same team! It could end the fear of war, the fear of pollution, and the fear of hunger and poverty. With all the money nations saved on preparing for war and defense, people's lives could be made more secure. Everyone could work together to improve the conditions of life on our planet.

This is not just a dream but a real possibility. All it takes is for people to change their way of thinking. It is encouraging and hopeful to see the beginning of this teamwork happening on the international scale, as countries come together to provide relief for nations suffering from disasters. The United Nations is a beginning of the idea of teamwork on a planetary scale.

Each of us can do our share by increasing cooperation in our own local environment: home, school, community, and amongst our friends and co-workers. The first step is to feel that you are part of a team, and then do your best to act for the good of the team.

3. Work to protect people and nature
When you understand that everything is life, you naturally work to protect life. *To protect life is to create the best conditions possible for all living things.* Different living things have different purposes and these must be respected.

Early man who collected his food was very much a part of nature. Like the birds and animals he could live off of nature's surplus, gathering the fruits of her wilderness. He made very little impact upon the whole life support system in which he lived.

Man's growth in numbers and creativity caused him to produce his food in great amounts. He also started to manufacture what he needed. These activities resulted in man feeling less a part of nature. As new purposes for natural resources developed, man lost sight of the necessity to maintain the balance of natural order. An example is in large scale agriculture. Because of the need and desire to produce food on a large scale, man developed chemical fertilizers and pesticides. Over the years, this has increasingly endangered the lives of other living things, including man himself.

All things live in a web of life. Birds ate insects and grains which had been sprayed with poison and then laid eggs that could not survive due to fragile shells. In 1963, for example, the Bald Eagle was reduced to only 420 adult pairs in all of North America. After banning the pesticide DDT, their numbers have increased to three thousand adult pairs today. The use of pesticides and chemicals in agriculture also damaged the health of farm workers and has polluted water supplies in many communities so that their water is no longer safe to drink for people or for animals.

If we protect nature, we will protect people and other living things. Understanding this will help repair the damage produced in the past by people who ignored the harmful effects of their practices. Protecting people and nature will be one of the most important jobs in the future and will influence how man uses nature in meeting his needs. Man cannot just meet his own needs thinking that he is separate from the life needs of other kingdoms of nature.

4. Work to improve the lives of others

After we learn how to live and work in such a way as to not harm people or nature, we must go a step further and work to improve the lives of others. In the past, we thought that to improve our life we only needed to develop *ourselves* and increase our *own* abilities and wealth.

❖

After understanding that

*we do not exist in isolation from others,
we realize that
our improvement
is tied to
the improvement of others.*

❖

There is even a greater key to self-improvement: *working to improve the lives of others is the most direct route to improving your own life.* Most people want most of all to be happy. Often people have sought their own happiness through gaining power, status, or many luxuries. They found out that these things in themselves did not bring happiness until they were used to help others. *Everyone has the ability to help others and gain happiness.*

❖

*Achieving the goal of happiness
does not depend on
what you have but
rather on how you use what you have.*

❖

Wealth, knowledge, happiness are different forms of life energy. When we work to improve life, we are working to increase the life energy in others. We want to help them be more active and optimistic and to set goals and reach them. When we give energy, we receive more energy in return.

Success, happiness, and fulfillment indicate the increase of life energy in us. When we all work to improve life, everyone is benefitted, and society increases in life energy. This will solve the problems of social and moral decay, escapism into drugs and crimes, and psychological and economic depression. All individual and social problems and diseases are the result of the absence of life energy circulating freely.

5. **Work for beauty**

There are many tales in world literature about how ugliness tries to defeat beauty but beauty — just by being beautiful — transforms ugliness into beauty. Like in the story *Beauty and the Beast,* Beauty is irresistible. Beauty is the true value in nature and in human nature. *All virtues are beautiful and they create beauty and health. Love, compassion, honesty, courage, purity, and dedication are noble values which inspire people and give them hope.*

When we work to spread these values in our life and in the lives of others, we become a source of beauty. We can actually purify the pollution which exists through negative people who try to bring us down. Beauty is irresistible. Beauty makes a person magnetic.

A great example in the modern age of the power of beauty is the life of Mother Teresa. A small, simple woman, acting alone to live a life of noble values through helping the poorest of the poor, has created an international organization. She has attracted money, workers, and many resources just because she is trying to create beauty where there is ugliness. Her work has affected people in every continent and has shown the beauty of the human spirit in action.

It is not beyond us to work for beauty. Everything we do, all of our actions, our attitudes, and gestures produce an effect upon ourselves and upon others. We have the choice to make ourselves and our surroundings beautiful or ugly. All the pollution, economic crises, and injustice in the world exist because people acted for selfishness, greed, hatred, fear, jealousy, and revenge. Ugly results are caused by ugly motives. *We have the power to create beauty by actions which show the noble values of the human spirit in every little thing we do.*

Sometimes we have chores which we don't like because they are dirty, take effort, or because we would rather do something else. If we do them with an attitude of helping others or with dedication; if we fill our thoughts with beautiful images; if we see the chore as an opportunity to create beauty in ourself and in our environment, the chore becomes a significant chance to improve.

Whenever we work for beauty, we are increasing the value of life. We are making everything more radiant with the energy of life, with the purpose of life. We discover the purpose of life when we work in beauty to produce beauty. The noble values are actually fine and beautiful lives because they are energies in the universe. Our actions enable these values to live and to do their work for humanity and for nature.

❖

*The role of each human being is
to demonstrate
the spirit,
energy,
consciousness,
or God in the universe.*

❖

I have seen teenagers transform their lives from boredom, negativity, and imitation or pseudo-rebellion to lives of excitement, enthusiasm, and purpose. They found a cause to work for — a cause which improves the lives of others. In working for their cause, they found love, they activated their noble inner values and made them alive. They became heroes in a real-life fairy tale in which they battled against ugliness, ignorance, and negativity.

The answer to the question "Is there life in other parts of the universe?" depends upon one's perspective. If we accept that life is energy, then life is everywhere and in everything. This question is only relevant and important if it makes us more aware of the importance of life. If it produces awareness and gratitude in us of the life with which we come in daily contact, then the question is significant. It is further significant if it makes us more inclusive and universal in our awareness, and makes us feel a greater kinship with other beings.

It is a person's unique responsibility in his or her own environment to increase life and to improve life. Degeneration and decay are epidemic in human society because people violate the laws of love and life. When people are cruel to each other, they are violating the basic unifying force which binds all beings together. It is really up to each person to ask him or herself if he or she is working for life. If one does not work to increase the life energy in others and to share the wealth of life energy, then life will be a miserable road to exploitation and death.

❖

*Life is a great gift
which each one of us must invest to
make it increase and show its glory.*

❖

CHAPTER III

FAILING IS NOT A RIGHT

Many times when I visit parks or walk nature trails I see beautiful trees wounded by people who have carved initials or symbols in the bark. It makes me so mad that people not only deface the beauty of nature, but also harm living trees.

I have had some students who have cut initials or symbols on their skin to make tattoos. Most of these students are intelligent, against violence and war, want to save the environment, and are compassionate for people who are disadvantaged or are victims of human rights abuses.

It bothered me that they were carving their skin, not so much for the sake of the skin but because of the reasons for which they did it. They are so sensitive to all the wrong in the world, to the problems and suffering, that they have become sucked up in it. They feel powerless, hopeless, and angry at the wrong in the world. They are expressing these feelings by literally wearing their rejection of the ugliness of society as a fashion statement. The carving of the skin, too, is a way of demonstrating that current society destroys beauty and nature. The irony is that these young people are "pacifists" and "ecologists." Yet they have not discovered how to creatively and constructively express their idealism.

Society is partially at fault for stifling their idealism and for smothering the flowers of youth with fear and degenerative images. Protest has become an obsessive fashion that is hiding the beauty of aspiration under a costume of dark despair.

I say society is *partially* at fault, because an individual still has responsibility and choice. There are examples of people who respond to social, political, and environmental corruption by trying to change and heal the wounds of this corruption and even to fight creatively against it. If a person chooses to become a victim of ugly exploiters and power mongers then they are becoming part of the problem instead of part of the solution. The "army" of goodness, peace, and light thereby looses some of its beautiful "soldiers."

I decided to talk to these students. I asked them if they loved trees. They did. I asked them why. They said that trees help the whole environment, providing food and shelter for animals, producing oxygen, helping to prevent global warming, and by adding beauty to the world. They are part of the web of life. I asked them if trees should be protected. They said that definitely they should be. Then I told them about some trees that had been carved and vandalized in a local park. Did they think that was a crime against nature? They thought it was an outrage by ignorant people. Then I asked them about carving their own skin. They were silent. Then they were confused. Then they became defensive. Then they understood.

❖

*Failure is going against a standard which you value.
Failure is not simply making a mistake but it is deceiving yourself.
It is disrespecting yourself.
It is building a false self either consciously or unconsciously.*

❖

Failure is betraying your goals and values. It is betraying the purpose for which you are alive. Every part of nature has a purpose, something positive to contribute to the environment, like a tree. Our chemistry is different, our energy is different, our sensitivity is different, our expression is different, but we have no less of a responsibility than does a tree: to be a contributing factor in the great web of life.

Some students excuse their failure by saying that it is their choice to fail. What they are saying is that they are free — that they could succeed if they wish, but that they are failing on purpose. They assert their independence in order to seem superior to the discipline and requirements of school. This is a great self-deception, like the fox who couldn't reach the grapes saying that they weren't ripe anyway.

Failing leads to dependence. People who fail never enjoy the freedom of being truly self-sufficient, and they have nothing to give. The reason for failing in the first place is because they are controlled by attitudes, habits, and desires which are against those which lead to success and freedom.

There are three types of people who fail.

The first type has a poor self-image. These people have been programmed for failure since birth. They have been abused, told they were worthless, criticized, and have not been given love. They live in environments where failure is acceptable and have no role model for success. They live in a state of dependency and feel they have nothing to give, no purpose for living.

The second type is just the opposite. They have been flattered and petted all their lives so that they have a selfish ego. They think that they are successful and don't need to make any effort. They are self-satisfied and think any effort to improve is stupid. They only do what they can do easily in order to show off. They only like people who flatter and praise them. They are also in a dependent state: they depend upon their state of satisfaction.

The third group is made up of people who have values, intelligence, and goals but never reach them. They don't reach them because they have fallen into the traps of attitudes, habits, or desires which have made them leave their goals. Sometimes they have become obsessed by temporary interests or fads, or they have become the victims of those who do not want them to succeed. These people develop character traits which go against their inner values. Sometimes they become dependent upon drugs or upon people who control them. These people are in a state of conflict because somehow they realize that they are living a false life. They try to justify their lives but weave greater webs of self-deception. These people become negative, depressed, defensive, or extremely ambitious. Their whole life becomes an effort to justify the false life they are living.

Those in group two and three may seem successful on the outside. They may even be rich, famous, and influential. However, if they are not true to themselves, they may be deemed failures and, privately, even *they* are aware of that. For example, you have many famous people, movie stars, entertainers, or financiers whose personal lives are a mess. They may be dependent upon alcohol or drugs, they may have unsuccessful marriages, rebellious children, or may be used by others. They are really lonely and have no true friends whom they can trust. They know people admire them for selfish reasons and that, because they are false, all their "friends" are false. So many people go through life like the beast in *Beauty and the Beast* with the ugly (or glamorous) false self covering their inner beauty and moral strength.

❖

*People cannot be happy or successful
if they live a false life.*

❖

Living a false life is failure. Being dependent is failure. Taking without giving is a sign of failure. Success is a life of integrity. Integrity is when your life activities, attitudes, and goals are a true reflection of your inner standards and noble values.

Since we live in an interdependent world and on a planet where nature provides the necessary conditions for life, no individual has the right to be a failure. Failing is not an expression of freedom or of free will. On the contrary, failing is an expression of ignorance, of dependency, of falsehood, of exploitation.

❖

*Nature did not provide for
any creature to be a failure.
In the scheme of nature,
living things become extinct only when
they fail to serve a purpose,
or when they become victims of those who
violate the purpose of nature.*

❖

Parasites exist in nature because they serve some purpose. However, all parasites belong to lower orders of life and are totally dependent, immobile, and unfree. People were not meant to be parasites! People were meant to be creative and supportive of life. Why else would humanity throughout the ages seek human rights which promote life, success, and achieving one's potential as a human being?

In all the declarations of human rights there is not one which states that an individual has the right to fail.

All rights are for human independence and to promote the common good. All over the world, people are fighting for their rights not to fail. They want adequate nutrition, they want love and respect, they want the rights of citizenship in a free society, they want freedom from exploitation, and they want to be educated to the maximum of their potential. People want to live a life which makes a contribution to the world, a life that has meaning.

Why do many young people in the United States, then, consider it their *right* to fail? They use drugs and alcohol, become slaves to their cars and clothes, working long hours to support them, become devotees of self-destructive "pleasures," become followers of the slogan "take it easy," and do not strive for excellence.

Part of the reason may be because they have been brainwashed by advertising. The fact that they *can* be brainwashed is because they are not given a higher vision of human purpose to use as a standard or goal in life. Additionally, they have not been encouraged to work for their rights, freedoms, and dignity. They take these gifts for granted, are not grateful, and become apathetic. The failure to exercise one's rights indicates a failure of the society to inspire its citizens.

We must ask why we have a social climate in which some people don't want others to be free and successful? Why has a youth culture developed which emphasizes satisfying all of one's desires while neglecting one's real, essential need for hope and for a future vision worth working for? Why have inner worth and virtue been devalued?

Young people need to resist and rebel against materialistic and selfish forces which are trying to program them for laziness and destruction. Young people must become activists to make life meaningful and creative for all people. They must be activists to secure the rights of success for all people. They must create for our society a positive vision of the future in which people are healthy, sane, and cooperate for the welfare of humanity.

❖

Rebellion for a better world in the future is to stand courageously for right and for the common good.

❖

CHAPTER IV

FREEDOM

The ultimate freedom is to fulfill one's purpose in life.

All people are seeking fulfillment on some level. If we look at all education, all politics, all arts, all sciences, and all religion; if we look at the work people do, we see that all the efforts are to find some meaning, some purpose, some fulfillment in life. A person cannot live without a reason for living. In freedom, the reason for living is the pursuit of a goal or a sense of responsibility. When people are not free, they act out of fear because fear forces them. They have no vision beyond basic survival or beyond the freedom from pain and suffering.

When we look at humanity today and throughout history, we must ask if there ever was a time when people were truly free! Even in the so-called "free" nations, people are dissatisfied and have fear. Many feel they have no power, no leadership, no worthy vision to hope and work for. History has been dominated by wars and selfish competition. Those few individuals who have reached some measure of fulfillment of their purpose have become the heroes of history.

❖

Actually, in all human beings there is some feeling that they, too, could be heroes if they had freedom.

❖

Heroism and freedom are the result of cooperating for a common goal that is not selfish but geared toward improving life. In natural disasters we see people working together to help each other. In fact, people may actually *like* disasters because they give them a chance to exercise their heroism. They give people a break from their daily routine in which they act automatically like machines. People's actions during disasters often remind us that heroism is possible.

People everywhere want the guarantee of certain basic rights and freedoms. They mainly want to live in freedom from fear and in freedom from being used by others. It is equally important, though, to have a common goal.

❖

Freedom from fear and pain are not sufficient to make life worth living. One must have goals.

❖

Goals by themselves, however, do not guarantee people freedom or fulfillment. The wars, problems, and misuse of power are the results of many goals. These are competing goals and selfish goals.

A problem in so-called "free" countries is that people chase selfish goals, and that many people have competing goals instead of common goals. A company may have a goal to sell cigarettes. So it spends millions and millions of dollars on advertising to get children to think that it is "cool" and exciting to smoke. In order for the cigarette company to achieve its goal, it must make people addicted to its product. In the meantime, the community in which the factory is located depends upon the factory for its economic stability. So the welfare of a business and of a community depends on making people slaves of its product. They live in fear of the factory closing if people become free of the smoking habit.

Another factory produces paper, a necessary product. However, the factory pollutes the river and the air in the community in which it is located. The people in the community do not fight the pollution for fear of hurting the factory which is their source of employment and enables them to buy what they need and want.

These examples show us that throughout nations and throughout the world, competing goals tie people in traps in which their existence depends on people having to give up their freedom.

❖

Goals must be based upon improving the welfare of humanity, upon making more people free.

❖

Goals must be the result of cooperation and the sense of responsibility. They must be geared for long-term success rather than for short-term pleasure.

For many young people, a feeling of great freedom comes when they are able to drive a car. They feel independent. A car for them symbolizes independence. Yet I have seen many young people for whom this turned into dependence. For example, I knew a young man who was a very good student, well above average. He was planning to go to a university after high school. When he started to drive, he bought a brand new, fancy 4 x 4 pickup truck with all the extras. Suddenly he had monthly payments, high insurance rates, gas, and upkeep to pay. He started working evenings and weekends in a fast-food place just to support his wheels. In his classes he was always tired, his homework was never done, he didn't concentrate, and his grades started going down. His poor grades in his junior and senior years ruined his chances to go to a university. He had the goal of having a 4 x 4, but this goal prevented him from reaching his purpose or from gaining skills he will need for an independent and prosperous life.

Many adults are the same way. In fulfilling their goals, they have created so much debt that they live in fear of their creditors. All they earn is for paying off their debts and for just surviving. Working to pay off the credit card is not a purpose for living. On the contrary, it makes life miserable.

❖

*Goals are like tools which
should help us reach our purpose.
When tools become our purpose,
then we have lost the meaning in our life
and the path to our true happiness.*

❖

Taking the example of the young man who became a "slave" to his 4 x 4, we may learn a lesson of adaptation or goal-fit decisions. Part of freedom is making right choices.

❖

*Right choices help us adapt to
necessity in the most efficient way
so that we can go beyond the necessity and
use our energy creatively.
Wrong choices waste our time, money, and
efforts, and take away our joy.*

❖

Wrong choices usually have to be undone with great effort, or else they lead us into a life style that drains all our energy and resources to support our wrong choices. Wrong choices waste our time, money, and efforts, and take away our joy. Recognizing that a vehicle is a necessity and an important tool to help us reach other goals, one needs to make a choice that fits one's circumstances and will not drain one's energy from one's real purpose. If the young man had chosen a good, older model 4 x 4, his expenses would have been much less. He could have managed maybe just working weekends and could still have kept up his grades. Eventually, after graduating from a university and getting a good job, he might have been able to afford his "dream machine."

❖

We observe that freedom is limited when we have goals which conflict with our purpose or when our goals become our "purpose."

❖

People voluntarily or involuntarily give up their freedom for the short-lived pleasure of a false goal or to be accepted. There are many forces in society which have the power to impose their values and goals upon us and thus take us away from our purpose, from our freedom. When we build our self-image according to others' values, we give up our freedom. We give them the power to control us, which usually means the power over our wallets and choices. We let ourselves be programmed by false images and conditioned by symbols.

Advertising exerts a great power over our ability to make free, independent choices.

It works upon that part of our nature that desires excitement, popularity, sex, possessions, and escape. It stimulates our desire for a glamorous life style, and tries to create in us a value system which makes happiness and self-esteem dependent upon buying, buying, buying. However, in its equation for happiness — *you + our product = happiness* — it doesn't stress the development of the character traits necessary to achieve success, much less freedom or independence.

Advertisers don't tell us the effect of their product upon our health or upon the health of the environment. They can't tell us the real cost of recreating the advertising life style in our life. They don't tell us the cost to our freedom. They just tell us that we've got to have it. In reality, marketing does not want people to be intelligent and independent. It starts programming us to be mindless consumers before we are old enough to develop independent judgment.

❖

A society that creates slaves in order to maintain its economic production and survival is a society headed for self-destruction.
A citizenry motivated by selfish consumerism and escapist pleasures will never be free, independent, or responsible.
❖

Conflicting pressures within society take away our freedoms by creating confusion and contradictory goals and values in our minds. For example, we are told on one hand to buy all kinds of things which create mountains of waste. On the other hand, we are told to conserve our natural resources because our planet is in danger. On one hand, we are excited by messages of a luxurious life — vacations, fancy cars, the latest fashions. On the other hand, we are told that debt is creating a crisis in our society, that people are losing their jobs and their homes, and that social problems and poverty are increasing in the world. On one hand, we are told to "take it easy," and "don't work too hard," so we live for the weekend. On the other hand, we are exhorted to be successful, productive, and to make our country competitive in the world market. *These mixed messages create such confusion that no matter what we do, we are doing wrong!*

We are pushed one way, then pulled another. Creating such conflict is an indication of a society which has no direction, no leadership, no standard or integrity. We are rafting on a wild river with no oars and no rudder. To save us from this destructive course, we need heroic, decisive, and responsible action.

❖

Instead of creating confusion, our leaders, our mass media, and our schools should promote

*free and responsible citizens
who will take heroic actions
to deal with our problems.*

❖

Heroes are fearless, compassionate, skillful, and serve the common good. Heroes are decisive because they have a value system in which they believe. They are decisive because they cannot be easily diverted from acting in accordance with their values.

A young man in our community saw a canoe capsize in icy flood waters. He immediately took action to save the occupants by plunging into the waters to bring the struggling victims inner tubes, and drag them to safety. Even though his father and other spectators tried to dissuade him, he took action. Authorities said that they would have died if they had been less than another minute in the water.

The qualities of heroism are directly related to our original definition of freedom: to fulfill one's purpose in life. Heroism is to have integrity, so that we live according to our highest values. Most of our actions are less dramatic than the above example, but they are equally heroic if they help us live according to our values. Resisting temptation and keeping our direction in the face of confusing appeals and pressures is heroic. With so many appeals from glamorous and false "freedoms," it is hard not to be side-tracked from our true purpose in life.

The first indication that we know our purpose is how we respond to the necessities of life. If we have a sense of responsibility both to ourselves and to others we will want to work to improve conditions. *If we are hungry and have only a couple of dollars to spend, do we buy food or do we buy a toy?* We do not only hunger for food for our body, but also for food for our soul. It is just as necessary to satisfy our spiritual hunger as to be well-fed.

❖

How often do we leave our soul starving while our body plays with its toys?

❖

The hunger of our soul can be satisfied by working to improve our life and the lives of others. When we respond to the necessities of life in such a way as to satisfy the hunger of our soul, we have no confusion. We have more joy, more hope, and we give joy and hope to others. We become leaders and heroes.

❖

When we live for our purpose, we cannot be tricked into wasting our resources, our time, and our energy by chasing after false images and temporary escapes.

❖

When we find our purpose in life, our soul is energized and we feel true freedom. We are no longer doubtful, depressed, guilty, uncertain, or frustrated, but are able to make clear, sane choices that help us reach the goals which are stepping stones to our purpose.

Knowing our purpose helps us work more efficiently and balance our work with enjoyable and fulfilling recreation. We have more time and resources because we use them purposefully. Then, both our work and our leisure are done with more joy, more creativity, and more energy. We develop a life style which is positive and which *we* control. All our activities — our work and our play — make a contribution to life. When we are in control, we are free.

❖

When we are in control of ourself,
we do not feel the need to control others.

❖

Most people want to control others because they, themselves, are unsatisfied. They use others to satisfy their egos. Because they are unable to control themselves, they deceive themselves into thinking they have power by trying to control and use others to satisfy their hunger. Freedom, on the other hand, makes others free. If you are free, you give an example to others and encourage others to be free. Your leadership blooms when you succeed in leading yourself to freedom. Think of the society which would emerge if all citizens were pursuing their purpose in life, becoming free, and encouraging others to become free!

❖

*Freedom is not just a promise
written in a bill of rights.
It is the quality of a life which unfolds
according to a plan of improvement.*

❖

Freedom is the result of nourishing your own soul and the souls of others with your joy, your positive attitude, your caring, and your desire to improve life. It is living with true goals, making goal-fit choices, and adapting to the needs of yourself and others with creativity and realistic purpose.

❖

*In the heart of every person is the
desire to be a leader.*

❖

To be a leader is to be respected, to be independent, to be knowledgeable, to be courageous in the face of difficulties, to have influence, to be able to help others, to have responsibility. When people look to us as a leader in something, when they ask our advice, it reinforces the feeling within our heart that we *are* somebody.

Our heart is connected to the life energy of the universe, to spirit. That spirit within our heart wants us to be free, to fulfill our purpose in life. When we lead ourself to freedom and are an example to others, then we become a leader. *All people are able to be leaders — to be examples of success, of self-determination, of living up to their potential, of overcoming difficulties in life.* Joy and success are contagious. People spread it like a fragrance wherever they go, giving others hope, making them free.

When humanity is in a miserable condition of despair; when people only live for economic survival, or when they live at the expense of other peoples' freedom to support their own; when people voluntarily become slaves to their "tools," to their luxuries, and to their "image;" they can easily be taken advantage of by unprincipled "leaders." In such conditions, leaders are needed who will act for real change out of a love for nature and humanity. One must become a leader with positive values to replace "leaders" with negative values. One must inspire others to act creatively and constructively for change which enhances freedom.

Often throughout history, leadership has been inspired by youth who are still sensitive to the urging of the spirit within their hearts. *Frequently it is the youth who are the conscience of a society, not just because they have a stake in the future, but because they try to awaken the society to moral truths.*

In recent times, young people have stood for protecting our environment, animals, and human rights when others were silent. Young people in many nations have stood fearlessly against the greed and insanity of war, to proclaim the values and vision of brotherhood. Such young people have been leaders, demonstrating the spiritual freedom which dwells in their hearts.

Note of Caution: When one begins to awaken to the realities of life and sees all that is wrong and that needs to be changed, one may feel the urge to change everything, but at the same time feel frustrated by one's lack of ability to do so. Two responses to this situation often occur:

First, a person may become openly rebellious and try to destroy all the wrong and expose the "evil."

Second, a person may become alienated from society, negative, apathetic, critical, self-righteous, and may want to drop out.

Both these reactions are counter-productive and full of traps which take away one's freedom. Both destructive rebellion and alienation can turn into self-centeredness or fads. They can become goals in themselves which prevent one from reaching one's purpose. By conforming to the style of rebellion rather than to the substance, one may isolate oneself and lose the power to influence others for constructive changes. Self-improvement, integrity in one's values, and service are the best ways to rebel against falsehood and injustice.

❖

*When one responds to challenges
creatively and tries to do whatever
one can do to improve life,
then he or she is on the path of freedom.*

❖

CHAPTER V

LIVING THE GOOD LIFE

Many fairy tales end, "and they lived happily ever after." To most people this is the conclusion most desired for the drama of life. Fairy tales are stories of challenge, of good against evil, of virtuous people who struggle against the cruel power of selfish or greedy ones, of shining heroes against ugly monsters. Fairy tales are stories of victories: of good-hearted compassion defeating sneaky tricksters; of simple honesty defeating treason, plotting, and lies; of courageous innocents overcoming evil forces.

Fairy tales represent a basic human drama. They reflect many of the psychological struggles of the human spirit against materialistic forces. They are often allegories of the inner struggle of people between the intentions of their virtues against the powerful desires of their vices.

Today, society is embroiled in this primal conflict on all fronts. Each side tries to win people's allegiance to its definition of "the good life." It is up to the individual to develop standards which serve as guidelines leading to the "good life."

It has been suggested here that virtues are such guidelines. It has also been suggested in previous chapters that working for the improvement of life, that working for goals related to one's purpose in life are paths to freedom, joy, and self-fulfillment.

❖

*In modern societies
the "Good Life" is defined by
either materialistic goals or spiritual goals.*

❖

Those who define the good life by materialistic standards emphasize HAVING. Those who define it by spiritual standards emphasize BEING. In other words, materialism says that the more one *has* the happier one is, while the spiritual side says that the more one *is* the more happy and fulfilled one becomes.

Each person has the desire to verify his or her own reality. How do people prove to themselves that they exist? The "good life" is a goal, a proof of existence, and a proof of worth as an individual. "Worth" usually means something permanent to people. Some people prove to themselves that they are of value, that their life is good if they receive much. Other people prove that their life is good if they give much.

For the materialistic standard of the good life, people feel they are worth the value of their possessions. Their self-esteem and reality consist of the value of their car, their house, their properties, their bank account, and other symbols of wealth. They identify themselves with their possessions and their life style. For a vast majority of those who seek this type of "good life," their life is a process of trying to satisfy their desires. However, a life driven by the desire to *have* is never satisfied. The result is a life of frustration, dissatisfaction, debt, and worry.

*The standard of the spiritual "good life" is **to give**.* One can only give what one has. However, people have more than just their possessions to give. People have a wealth of qualities such as love and compassion, helpfulness, leadership, ideas, and skills to improve the common good, creativity, the desire to save others from their misery and hardship. People who give never feel poor. They don't doubt their self-worth or their existence.

In the process of giving one's best and serving others, one touches the permanent center of one's being. One discovers the treasure chest of one's spirit. The jewels of one's spiritual self multiply when one gives. These jewels are one's virtues and one's intelligence. These gifts lead inevitably to a successful life.

❖

Fulfillment is continuing progress.

❖

People seek fulfillment from life. Without the hope of fulfillment, why do people live? What if you stopped your development when you were ten years old? Physically, emotionally, and mentally you would not be fulfilled. Your world would be very small, you would be dependent upon others, you would have little responsibility. You would not experience the joy of life. When you are ten years old, the concept of progress and the thirst for some destination are very real. You know that there is more to learn, more potential to develop, that there are more experiences to be had. You want to become an adult, you want to have a role to play in life as a worker, a parent, a participant in society. Nature provides the impulse to grow physically, emotionally, and mentally, and society provides the stimulus for developing traits and qualities of body, emotion, and mind which shape your personality and self-image.

Being an adult and having a personality do not, in themselves, bring fulfillment, however. This is because an individual has a greater destiny than adulthood. Adulthood is just a stage of physical, emotional, and mental development like any stage, with its knowledge, rights, and responsibilities. Yet, to feel that there is no higher destination nor more growth possible is as ridiculous a concept as to stop growing when you are ten years old!

Sometimes we can observe people who think they have "made it" in life. They know how to make and spend money and all the "right" ways to impress people. They know how to hold their knife and fork, how to order wine and drink it, how to smile and wink knowingly, how to talk with enthusiasm about nothing of real importance. Their life is a life of parading their egos, exciting their senses, and exerting their power like emperors. Yet for one who is seeking spiritual fulfillment, such emperors have no clothes! They are spiritually naked, and spinning like wooden tops in one place until they fall down. Their lives are adult versions of children's dress-up play.

This ridiculous play is the model of the "purpose of life" which is perpetuated by all the glamorous image makers in the market place. It is the popularized version of "success" and "fulfillment" which motivates so many people. However, it is sad that such goals cement people's development at a childish stage of existence and make them dependent upon exciting toys. Such people's lives become empty of meaning. They can be controlled by those who know how to play upon their desires. This is sad because it goes against nature and leads people away from natural growth and development into a fulfilled human being.

❖

To want to be important and unique, to want to be SOMEBODY is a natural impulse.

❖

The natural impulse to be fulfilled comes from the very force of life circulating throughout our bodies. If our hearts and minds are not asleep, this impulse puts us in contact with the world of knowledge; it builds bridges of communication; it brings out our capacity to love and our desire to nurture others. When our life force, our love, and our intelligence are coordinated and directed toward a noble purpose for the improvement of life, we become creative and we become leaders.

❖

*The main difference between
materialists and
those who seek spiritual fulfillment
is how they use their energy and wealth
and view their destination.*

❖

If materialists achieve success, their success inflates their ego and stimulates their body and mind. Body and mind serve their selfish interests and freeze their progress in a spiritual sense. Materialists become obsessed with image, wealth, and power. These symbols of success replace the urge to improve and to serve. Such people often seem happy and energetic; their power and influence seem irresistible, but they are mostly driven by the desire to have more or by the fear of losing what they have. Such "successful" people lose their inner peace and do not experience the joy of life. The symbols of success have replaced the beauty of life and the expanding communication with the life force of humanity and nature.

Since people naturally seek to be "somebody," what are the spiritual counterparts of material success? While materialists develop image, wealth, and power to serve themselves, people who work for spiritual fulfillment develop *nobility, creativity, and leadership* in order to serve others. When people develop the qualities of spiritual fulfillment, they become wealthy as a consequence of their spiritual success. Nevertheless, this wealth does not become their goal in life, nor does it become their self-image.

Nobility radiates the virtues and expressions of the inner light throughout all of a person's being. A noble person has grace, beauty, joy, and solemnity and radiates an energy which uplifts and attracts people. This is real and not put-on; it is natural and free from ego.

Creativity is an energy of enthusiasm for one's study or work. It is tuning in with the plan and purpose of life and then using one's insight, knowledge, and skills to express that purpose. Creativity is like plugging yourself into the electric current and transforming that energy with your unique qualities into an "appliance" that meets a special need.

Leadership is the example one sets for others and it is one's field of service. The greater one's field of service, the greater a leader one becomes. A person can be a leader in any relationship one has. Such people become wealthy not only in money, but also in property and in co-workers. However, they use all their wealth to help fulfill their purpose and to benefit the lives of others. Great philanthropists are examples of this.

❖

Nobility, creativity, and leadership are more powerful even than happiness.

❖

Happiness is important but not essential for self-fulfillment. Many people reach fulfillment in the trials and pains of crises. Sometimes crises test our soul and cause us to tap inner resources we never thought we had. *Once we have a moment in which we experience some of our hidden potential, our life changes.* One success in a critical situation, one difficult test passed can change our life. Some crises reveal whom we can trust.

❖

Happiness is temporary satisfaction, but nobility, creativity, and leadership are inner states of focus which release our energy, our enthusiasm, and our potential.

❖

Creative people and leaders do not use happiness as a measure of success. People who use noble values as their standard are motivated by their ideals and sense of responsibility. Such people have a reason for living and enthusiasm for life. On the other hand, the constant search for personal happiness often results in dissatisfaction, frustration, pain, and suffering.

How is this so? This is so because if personal happiness is your goal, you can never reach it to your satisfaction. Two factors cause dissatisfaction when you seek satisfaction.

First, a peculiarity about desire is that the more you try to satisfy it the more it wants. Desires can control you. Eventually you reach a point of saturation in which you reject or even hate that which you desired. Your whole life will be a search for more happiness because you will be dissatisfied by not having, dissatisfied by being a slave to your desires, or else dissatisfied by having too much. A person for whom pleasure is a major motivation has difficulty being satisfied.

Second, in seeking personal happiness you are seeking something which is limited by its very nature. In trying to experience more happiness, you become more selfish and more isolated. You cut yourself off from the energy of love which is only maximized by caring for others and by giving. In its extreme, seekers of personal happiness often hurt themselves and others. In the end they feel more unhappy, lonely, bitter, jealous, and suspicious.

The most important success is to have good relationships. This begins with one's family and friends and expands ever outward. *The greatest resource for building good relationships is a loving heart, a giving heart.* In a relationship one must not be selfish. In friendship, marriage, family, and even in business, relationships should not be commercial transactions governed by selfish interest. A person must serve others, complete others as they complete you. We all become greater, more prosperous, more creative, energetic, and free as we give to each other. We multiply each other's energy, joy, hope, creativity, and sense of purpose as we give and encourage others. This can only be proven by doing it. If more and more people do it, goodwill, peace, and prosperity will increase in the world!

❖

People have been conditioned to want more and more as they search the key to the good life. They often seek to express themselves through their possessions.

❖

The thirst for personal happiness is stimulated because people are unhappy and dissatisfied in their lives and relationships. They package themselves, hoping to be attractive to others like fancy presents. However, eventually others discover that the pretty wrappings may cover an empty box with no gift inside.

People seek personal happiness to get out of their emptiness and fear. It is tragic that the image makers of society perpetuate that emptiness and fear in order to sell their pre-packaged "good life." Powerful materialists control the psychology of people, making them seek pleasure and avoid pain. This is the way animals are trained to be obedient to their masters. It is unfortunate that this behavioral conditioning controls most people's motivation even in such important areas as those of education and human relationships. *What we learn and what we love has been shaped in order to make us good consumers and devoted workers in non-essential industries.* This prevents us from making the greatest possible discovery, the discovery of our true Self.

❖

*The artificial "good life"
is a danger to
the survival of freedom,
human culture,
and the environment.*

❖

Only by developing one's human potential through education and service can one express one's nobility, creativity, and leadership. The "good life" may be based upon personal goals and values, but an individual will not experience it to the fullest unless others are able to experience it also. If people seek the fulfillment and expansion of joy and wisdom, then life will improve for everyone. *People must be like fearless explorers pursuing greater destinations. Like the heroes in a fairy tale, we must conquer the evil which tries to trap us and keep us from our quest.* Our inner strength and the power of our virtues will keep us going and help us conquer the monsters on our path to a life that is good for ourselves and for others.

CHAPTER VI

FINDING THE PATH

The "path" is a symbol of our travel through life during which we gain experience, insight, and development. There is a dimension of time on the path which marks physical growth and development, emotional growth, and mental growth. This is automatic "growing up." It is mostly unconscious and is conditioned by the situation in which we were born: nationality; culture; parental, family, and social influences.

❖

*Each person encounters challenges,
positive and negative experiences,
successes, and failures.
All these are for the purpose of
bringing us to a point psychologically when
we are ready to be independent
and to shape our future.*

❖

Sometimes in our childhood and youth we feel that we are at the mercy of blind forces. Before we can begin our path to the future, we have to be able to separate our habits, prejudices, and false images from the qualities which we feel represent our real, true Self. It is hard to travel the path with excess baggage of automatic, unconscious behavior. While physical, emotional, and mental growth is affected by time, we also have a timeless dimension which is the development of our soul which is infinite. Signs indicating our soul qualities are the virtues we have developed, our special talents, the positive heroes who inspire us, the ideals by which we try to live, and our highest goals in life.

At the beginning of the path, we often see two parallel or simultaneous paths in our life. Sometimes these are compatible, sometimes they create some friction. One path represents our personality life which adapts to the needs, expectations, and requirements of life. Much of our personality is shaped by our desires, especially by the desire to be liked and to belong to a group of some kind. Other parts of our personality path result from values or attitudes that have been programmed into us. Our personality is also formed by how we have chosen to express our talents and individual character traits.

The other path is our soul path, our spiritual destiny, our potential. When our personality activities reinforce our inner values and are in harmony with our purpose in life, these two paths are mainly one path with one direction. Our energy is focussed and we have integrity. Friction develops when our personality activities contradict our purpose in life. This is very common, and the friction causes us to want to change, or else we live in constant conflict and misery.

Our inner purpose is like a sieve. Life shakes us until only the right activities pass. Our purpose is our true motivation in life, what we live for, how we use our energy. It is not unusual for people to be swept along the personality path and lose their inner direction. Our personality can be controlled by outer forces which encourage our false self, our ego, to grow.

In such a condition, the choices we make and the friends we choose set up a chain reaction of results which sometimes create a mess of obligations. These may limit our freedom and future choices. I know many teenage mothers who have had to drop out of school or who have been delayed for many, many years from fulfilling their careers. Many never married, leaving their dream of love and family unfulfilled.

No matter how far we may stray from the path of our soul, the sieve of life will shake us from time to time, creating opportunities or crises which make us want to change and to leave the coarse trash of our past mistakes or false personality behind. These times of shaking are milestones in our life when we can take a new direction more in harmony with our soul.

❖
*As we succeed in integrating the
path of our personality with
the path of our soul,
we feel increased energy and motivation,
we make new plans,
and feel more happiness.*
❖

When we begin a new direction, we feel our life is in gear and we have the urge to develop new skills to achieve new goals. We discover our self-discipline, our abilities, and we encounter people and situations that provide opportunities for success. When we integrate our personality goals and activities with our purpose in life, we feel like we have a helper in life. We feel luckier, we get breaks; we meet people who help us, encourage us, who are trustworthy friends. We feel freer, liberated from past chains of people, of behavior, and of past programming.

I had a student who had terrible problems which she had largely created herself. She could not get along with anyone in her family or in school except for her special friends. She developed a problem with alcohol abuse, dropped out of school, and caused much pain to her loved ones.

After several years of no contact, I suddenly received a Christmas card and letter from her. She informed me that she has conquered her problems now. She is preparing to enter a university having finally gotten a certificate of completing high school requirements. Her goal is to become a psychologist. She is happy and full of energy. Although unaware of the details of her trials and rehabilitation, I am so happy and encouraged by the positive tone of her recent letters to me.

Here is an excerpt of a letter I received from her:

> "Hi, you might have a few questions running through your head. The first one might be who is this. The second might be why is she writing me this now. Well this letter I felt must be sent.... A couple of years have passed by now, and I feel I owe you an apology and it's sincere. I can't live with the past until I make amends with the ones I've hurt. If you'll accept my apology it would make me feel so much better. If you don't accept my apology I'll understand. You tried to help me out, and finally after all this time I realized that.... Well now, I'm apologizing for my behavior. And it's sincere. I've shaped up. I have my G.E.D. diploma, I also have a job. Next year I want to sign up for a few classes at NAU. Then I'll be ready to indulge in my education and respect the ones who teach...."

We take the first step in finding our path when we establish a clear direction in our life which is compatible with our soul's purpose. We have more understanding of ourselves and others, we want to be successful, and we want to be of greater service to others.

❖

*How do we know
when we are entering our true path?*

❖

First of all, we feel no inner conflict such as doubt, loss of energy, or depression, guilt, irritation, or self criticism. We have a clear conscience whose voice tells us we're on the right track. We become more happy, more optimistic, and have a positive mental outlook.

Second, we start to get new ideas, make new plans, and feel more power and creativity.

Third, we start taking actions which improve our life. This begins the process of changing our image to fit more closely our new self concept and purpose. We make decisions which will help us break unwanted habits and relationships. We see new skills we wish to develop, and we decide to educate ourselves.

Fourth, we see an improvement in our relationships with our family, with people we work with, and we make new friends.

Fifth, our new vision for our future opens up new possibilities. *Almost magically we meet people who help us or introduce us to people who can help us. New opportunities present themselves and we are ready to take them.* Our sense of purpose and self-confidence give us more daring to take risks.

Finally, we find ourself being more attractive and magnetic for those people and resources which will help us and encourage us to reach our goal.

❖

*When we find our path and
start to adapt to a
new direction,
we do not become free of crises in our life.*

❖

In spite of new crises, we are better able to cope because we have a vision of our future and we are more able to deal with crises in a positive way. Crises come from a variety of sources.

First, *when we decide to change, all those old habits, old friends, and old forces that were controlling us in the past rebel against our new direction and try to stop us from changing.* They needed us and depended upon us for their nourishment. So when we decide to change, they cause problems for us. They become our enemies and try to attack us. Rather than attacking us outright, however, they use methods which confuse us, weaken our determination, cause self doubt, appeal to our physical or emotional pleasures, our vanity and ego. Sometimes they try to tempt us with goodies, sometimes they spread gossip, sometimes they appeal to our pity and emotions to make us feel guilty.

❖

*Just because we decide
to change and improve,
the results of past choices and past actions
are not suddenly erased.*

❖

Another source of crisis is the wrongs we did in the past. Everything we do, whether good or bad, sets in motion a chain of events. It is hard to undo relationships which we see as wrong because relationships can be like traps holding us to our past. If we hurt people and said things we now regret, we have to heal those wounds. If we committed "crimes," we have to pay for them or else be forgiven. We may have made choices that now will take great efforts to correct or which caused us some damage. We may have given people a negative or false attitude about us. *It is difficult to change our image in people's minds and change their expectations about us.* This creates still more frustration and trials for us.

A third source of crisis is the gap we see between what we are and what we want to become. It takes time and effort to achieve our vision. This crisis is a crisis which tests our determination and commitment.

Finally, there is a crisis created by success. This is so subtle a crisis because it is disguised as happiness and self-satisfaction. If we have some success, sometimes we develop ego and pride. We want to show off, and we think we have made it. We stop striving to improve.

This crisis demonstrates that our basic motivation for improvement was selfish. We become satisfied and stop our growth and do not realize our purpose in life beyond personal success.

❖

It is our vision and determination to follow a path of improvement and service which gives us strength and guidance to face these crises.

❖

The virtues of our soul give us the tools to meet crises. We are able to rise above crises and learn from them how to build right relationships. We have a new attitude toward the challenges of life, many of which we, ourselves, created. We learn the power of love, forgiveness, commitment to values. We develop patience, tolerance, and understanding. We gain the power to let go of the past. We develop an open mind and defeat fear, doubt, and prejudice. We gain faith in our inner strength and in the power of virtue. We become honest with ourselves and with others. We gain the power and joy which come from following the path of our purpose. We live to serve others and not ourselves.

❖

Just as there are negative forces activated and put in motion against us because of wrong actions in the past, there are also positive forces which are activated by our good motives and deeds, and these help us achieve.

❖

We also get help in our crises and battles from new friends, from new teachers, and even from strangers who come to us with the right advice or with help when we need it. Whether we attract enemies or helpers depends upon our own magnetism.

Most people experience a "gut feeling" of attraction or repulsion for certain people, places, music, films, events, images, and so forth. Sometimes we go by these feelings and sometimes we ignore them. *When we are hypnotized, programmed by publicity or by desire, we loose our natural response of attraction or repulsion.* When we ignore our natural responses, our value system is out of order, our magnetic compass is broken.

I remember when I was very young I delivered newspapers at 4 o'clock in the morning to every house in a neighborhood. In the silence of the morning, I was very sensitive to the feeling of each home. Beyond their physical appearance I felt that some were places of happiness while others were places of suffering and meanness. At the end of the month, I had to go to each house to collect a voluntary payment for the paper. Some houses I totally avoided, they repulsed me so. My instincts about each house were verified by the occupants. Sometimes I forced myself to overcome my repulsion for certain houses out of curiosity. After ringing the bell, I waited in fearful expectation. If they didn't answer, I left relieved. However, those who answered verified my "gut feeling." They were mean, abusive, complaining, and unhappy people. Some were evidently alcoholics.

We often experience these same "gut feelings" about people or places. We know when people will be good for us or take us into trouble. Nevertheless, either out of curiosity, the desire for excitement, the desire to do something "forbidden," the desire to hurt ourselves or others, or because our compass is out of order we ignore instinctive warnings.

❖

*When we want to follow
the path of our purpose in life,
we must be free of
outer, conditioning forces
and read our compass accurately.*

❖

Our path results in increasing our service to others and opens another dimension in the magnetic law. As previously described, we all have instinctive protective feelings of attraction or repulsion which are to guide us as we stumble blindly through life. When we have purpose and specific goals for improving our lives and the lives of others, our eyes open and we have definite, conscious standards by which we make choices. This is conscious discrimination, logic, control over our desires, and listening to our inner voice.

❖

*Our actions and intentions
attract people and opportunities
and repulse certain dangers
or harmful situations.*

❖

The law of attraction and repulsion is not just a warning system, but it is also a major cause of what happens in our life. Knowingly or unknowingly, people are always the cause of their circumstances due to this law. We commonly call this "luck." We know people who always have bad luck, are accident prone, or always sick; people who are always having personal problems, who get into bad relationships, who get into trouble, who get into fights, who get ripped off, or are victims of assault. Sometimes it is hard to face the fact that we reap whatever we sow.

However, once we develop discrimination and watchfulness over our motives and actions, the law of attraction and repulsion then begins to operate on a different level. We consciously become the causes of attraction and repulsion. Our actions and intentions attract people and opportunities and repulse certain dangers or harmful situations.

Our thoughts, feelings, intentions, and actions are our magnet. The more they are influenced by our life's purpose or by the qualities of our soul, the more they have the power and magnetism of our soul. This magnetism brings us in contact and relationship with others with similar magnetism and repels those whose magnetism is coarser or not in harmony with ours. Since our relationships and friendships are built upon the qualities of our magnetism, it is important that we direct our thoughts, feelings, and actions toward our soul purpose. This then removes obstacles.

I know a very beautiful young woman who has high spiritual and humanitarian values and goals. Her beauty has attracted some very high quality friends. However, she has a few "bugs" in her, such as vanity and the desire for influence or power over others. She is also attracted to lower psychic phenomena and magic. She is aware of her attractiveness and sexuality and sometimes uses them to manipulate others. These "bugs" have polluted her purity. The pure light of her spiritual path had spots of decay. Like a pearlescent tooth with a cavity, her vices may become a breeding ground for germs which may cause her much pain and suffering. Her "bugs" have also caused her to attract people with degenerate and evil intentions who want to obsess and control her. Cultists and black magicians are attacking her. She is deceiving herself by fighting back, using similar tactics as her attackers.

This is an example of how our thoughts, feelings, intentions, and actions create our relationships for good or for evil. By fighting her attackers on their level, she is lowering her magnetic vibration to their coarseness.

Even though she is "fighting back," she unknowingly is becoming like them. She is building a relationship with them while at the same time diminishing the beautiful vibration of her soul qualities and goals. The only way she can repulse them and protect herself while keeping her integrity is to ignore them and increase the expression of her virtues and values. The high qualities of her soul are her best protection. Doing good for others selflessly will shield her. The evil thoughts of her attackers will bounce and return to the senders. Like the saying goes, "He who spits at heaven gets spit in his own face."

This young woman is in danger because of the conflicting pulls of her spiritual path and her personality path or ego. If she falls to her attackers, she will also bring her beautiful friends with her because of her magnetism and influence. Her only hope is to increase her light, love, and selfless service to others. She must exert extra effort to maintain her integrity with her spiritual values.

❖

*Our desires, our egos,
our needs, and programming
create a magnetic attraction for
people and situations which tempt us away
from our spiritual focus.*

❖

Her case is not unusual. All of us as we grow up have spots of decay which attract "germs." Peer pressures and social pressures have more effect upon us if we do not have a vision and goals for the future. Materialistic life uses goal-less people as food, consuming their time, energy, money, and beauty to satisfy its urges for power, sex, and luxury. This has created an overpowering materialistic cult in all modern societies today and has constructed its own "big picture." People fit into this puzzle of life or resist it according to the magnetic law of attraction and repulsion.

HELP ON THE SPIRITUAL PATH

❖

Just like a school where we progress from kindergarten through high school, the path of life leads from simpler lessons to more complex ones.

❖

When we respond more and more to the values and urgings of our spiritual nature, we attract those who may help us along the path to the fulfillment of our purpose. As we progress through the "school of life," our tasks become more complex. As our abilities develop, our responsibilities, goals, and influence become more serious. So just like a progressing student, we need guidance and help. We will also become a source of guidance and help for others. Just as we attract those who will help us because of our values and striving, we will attract those whom we can help through our desire to use our abilities in service to others.

❖
*Our first source of guidance will be
our own Inner Guide.*
❖

The Inner Guide is the voice of our conscience — the qualities and standards of our most noble virtues. As we grow up, we are protected and guided by our parents, teachers, and religious leaders who reinforce our conscience. They give us values, they support us through our successes and failures, and they prepare us for independence the best way they know how. Once we reach a certain point of maturity, *we* become responsible. We discover that all our guides throughout childhood were not perfect — nor are we. We must be grateful for their efforts and demonstrate our gratitude by continuing to grow and by nurturing and increasing the good seeds they planted.

❖
*Like a student progressing through school,
we must always be ready to
move on to the next grade;
we must not become stuck with
comfortable, old lessons,
knowledge, and teachers
but move on to higher levels.*
❖

As we develop more serious needs, we will meet more serious teachers. Our questions about the purpose of life and our sincerity to be a contributing part of the great puzzle of life will attract people, experiences, and books that will teach us. Like a student progressing through school, we must always be ready to move on to the next grade; we must not become stuck with comfortable, old lessons, knowledge, and teachers but move on to higher levels. We can only thank our teachers by increasing our beauty, wisdom, and service, and "graduate" to higher achievements and higher teachers.

❖

True spiritual teachers have certain qualities which separate them from frauds.

❖

As we travel the spiritual path, we need spiritual teachers. We must, however, be cautious of frauds. We can distinguish a true spiritual teacher from a fraud by definite and distinct qualities. A real teacher

1. encourages independence
2. does not infringe upon your freedom
3. challenges you to improve
4. never flatters you
5. does not impose beliefs, books, or ceremonies
6. serves selflessly his or her students and others
7. is an example of what he or she teaches
8. does not make claims nor shows off about personal achievements or "powers"

9. encourages students to be successful in their practical life
10. does not force students to progress but instead gives vision of future possibilities
11. stands for unity and appreciation of all peoples, races, and religions
12. promotes clear thinking, right relationships, and responsibility
13. emphasizes that spiritual progress is for the purpose of serving humanity and nature
14. discourages the worship of personalities including him or herself
15. never makes demands upon a student's person or property

❖

If we keep these standards in mind as we seek guidance along our path, we will never fall into the traps of cults nor become devotees of frauds.

❖

People who are seeking to expand their awareness in spiritual matters, to find more self fulfillment, and to serve others are vulnerable to appeals of false "teachers." Their virtues of idealism, trust, faith, and goodwill make them easy prey to people who know the right bait to use. Healthy skepticism and definite standards are needed to avoid being misused by people and organizations with selfish motives. The above list of standards will help us avoid being taken in by frauds who want to lead us to a dead end, detour our spiritual progress, and make us abandon our responsibilities and purpose in life.

❖

Anything you do with a sense of purpose is a spiritual activity.

❖

When we pursue our purpose in life, we will naturally awaken and develop our inner potentials. Many people feel that their spiritual life is separate from their day-to-day life. They think that it is necessary to set aside a special time for spiritual things after using most of their time working to pay their bills. This is false thinking. It is your attitude and motivation which make work spiritual or not. In any work we can strive to serve and strive for perfection.

❖

Liberation is the fruit of serving others and creating right relationships.

❖

It is absolutely necessary that within our family, work, and community relationships we strive for liberation of ourselves and of others. When we have dishonesty, conflict, or selfishness in a relationship, we weave a sticky web which traps us and others with threads of distrust, hatred, jealousy, revenge, disloyalty, competition, fear, ungratefulness, and apathy. Trying to get out of this web is a nightmare, unless we can cut the threads with the sword of our spiritual values and striving.

❖

The spiritual life is the result of fulfilling our career and family responsibilities with the purpose of bringing out the potential treasures of the spirit within every person and within every form.

❖

As we fulfill our material needs, we must have a purpose beyond them. We want our life to contribute to the planet and to humanity. This may demand from us a spirit of sacrifice, for the future may present many unpleasant yet essential jobs. As in changing a baby's diaper, *we will have to be like loving parents to clean up the social and environmental messes on our planet.* We must not do our duties just because we feel forced to or because of our material needs. We must see them as opportunities to improve our life and the lives of others.

❖

The spiritual path is not traveled alone. Our achievements may help others to achieve.

❖

CHAPTER VII

FRIENDSHIP, LOVE, MARRIAGE, AND SEX

A true friend will always lift you up, never bring you down.

A friend is encouraging and looks out for your best interests. Understanding these fundamentals of friendship, beware of so-called "friends" who want you to do things against your values, or who play with your emotions in order to control you. Many people enter into "friendship" in order to satisfy their own needs and egos. False friendships are always based upon selfishness while true friendships are based on love.

❖

True friendship makes us want to improve,
it gives us optimism,
helps us to bloom, and
gives us a hope for the future.

❖

Everyone wants to have friends. We want to love and to be loved. We want to develop relationships which inspire us and lead us to greater happiness, greater achievements, greater fulfillment in life. Friendship builds us because it calls forth many of our soul qualities such as compassion, generosity, tolerance, patience, and responsibility. In return we gain confidence, self-esteem, support, and faith. True friendship makes us want to improve, it gives us optimism, helps us to bloom, and gives us a hope for the future.

❖

*Alone we are a random puzzle piece
without meaning,
but as we gather friends around us,
our purpose in life comes into focus.*

❖

Friendship affirms our place in the great puzzle of life. When we fit in the right place in the jigsaw puzzle, the interlocking pieces which surround us are our friends. They enable us to complete the picture as we help them also complete it. In friendship we become complete and whole. We are able to contribute our qualities to the big picture. Alone we are a random piece without meaning, but as we gather friends around us, our purpose in life comes into focus.

We can add here another definition of friendship: friendship is the relationship of people who have the same goal or purpose in life. Common purpose forms a bond which helps us reach fulfillment.

❖

The standards of friendship form

the foundation of love and marriage.

❖

Marriage is a commitment of friendship. It is the recognition that your friend and you will work together to fulfill your goals. It is a recognition that you have a responsibility to help another fulfill his or her purpose in life. In a successful marriage, your partner will be a true friend. A true friend will be honest with you, help you achieve your goals, and help you to overcome your obstacles.

❖

One of the great mysteries and great expectations in life is how we may find our "True Love."

❖

People look for love in many places and in many ways and end up disappointed or hurt. Some find short-lived, even damaging relationships.

A young woman student once angrily exploded, "I hate boys! They're mean and you can't trust them! They don't know how to treat a girl!" This was an intelligent and pretty girl. However, the way she dressed was just an advertisement for sex. I asked her what kind of a young man she was looking for. She replied that she wanted someone who respected her, was intelligent, fun to be with and whom she could trust. I said, "To catch such a fish you have to use the right bait!" She laughed and said, "Be serious!" "I am serious. If you fish for catfish who live in the mud, you have to use rotten bait and fish in the mud. You are using the wrong bait to catch the kind of fish you want. You are using your body as bait so you will attract those who just want a body. To find a young man who will be true to you, you have to be true to yourself."

Slowly she began to change her image, the way she dressed, her make-up. Her language and expressions changed. She quit smoking. She became more serious about studying. Gradually I noticed her friends changing and I noticed she became involved in school activities. At the beginning of her senior year, she came to me for a letter of recommendation. "I decided to go fishing at the university." We both laughed. Then I said, "That's great! They have the biggest catfish there! Watch out!" She pretended to look hurt, then she smiled. "Come on, you know I'm not fishing for catfish!" She gave me a big hug with great joy.

❖

What we want out of a relationship is what we get.

❖

It is tragic that so many friendships and marriages fail. Often these are the result of people using the wrong bait and fishing in the wrong waters. If we want to find our "soul mate," then we have to express our soul qualities. What we want out of a relationship is what we get. The law of attraction works throughout our life. The path that we follow will take us to those places where we will meet our friends.

We saw in the previous chapter how the law of attraction and repulsion works in our life. As we create our magnetism, we create the chemistry in our life which forms our relationships. The quality of our magnetism determines the quality of our relationships and opportunities.

❖

We can be builders of dynamic, beautiful, and creative relationships.

❖

The forces of nature want us to be successful. They urge all life toward greater unity and cooperation. Life is an ecological system in which all parts work together for health, nourishment, and progress of the whole. We can cooperate and do our part in this system to make it more dynamic, more beautiful, and more creative. We can be builders of dynamic, beautiful, and creative relationships. When we cooperate in this way, all the elements will cooperate with us, making us more dynamic, beautiful, and creative. This is the give-and-take ecology of life in which we live. This is the basis for friendship. When we do our part with enthusiasm, with deep concern for the welfare of other parts, without expectation for personal reward, and with the desire to create unity we are expressing love.

There are many beautiful stories of the power of love. Recently I saw a fourteen year old girl on television who gave $1,600 from her college account to help a boy who needed an eye operation. She had met him at a rally to support an anti-drug program in their community. When she learned that he needed an operation and that his family could not afford it, she decided that she would give some of her savings. She explained that he was helping a cause she believed in and she wanted to help him.

❖

Love is the creative expression of the law of attraction.

❖

    Magnetic attraction results in the flow of energy between all elements in nature. It keeps life circulating and is a constructive force. The very atoms which are the building blocks of matter interact due to their magnetic chemistry. Within the atom itself are positive and negative charges which make its energy system. Atoms build their relationship with other atoms to create molecules and more complex systems. This electromagnetic power is part of the spirit which circulates throughout the universe. It is the expression of the love energy in matter.

    Electricity flows because of magnetic attraction. We see on batteries and other systems a positive and negative pole. Without this polarity there would be no magnetic interchange, no electricity. In all creative activities is this urge to bridge the gap between opposites: between spirit and matter, between idea and expression.

❖

By understanding that we can build our magnetic quality as a consequence of our values, goals, and choices, we can comprehend the special gift of being human.

❖

Human beings are part of this energy system. If we view ourselves as atoms or cells in this system, we see our responsibility and creative power in a new light. We can see in a less abstract or metaphoric way that we really are pieces in a great jig-saw puzzle! We can clearly understand the importance of the quality of our magnetism. We can comprehend the special gift of being human: that we can build our magnetic quality as a consequence of our values, goals, and choices; that we can know where we fit by using our energy to express the qualities of our Soul.

❖

The energy of life is a precious, sacred energy, responsible for unifying the different parts of nature into creative relationships. This energy produces the wealth and abundance which support life.

❖

One form of this precious energy is sexual energy. Like all other expressions of spiritual energy, it has an important purpose. Sex is a basic creative energy in the universe, just like the flow of electricity between poles in a battery. Between a man and a woman, sex can be a unifying, constructive force — an expression of love and common purpose. It is sad and a dangerous waste of creative energy that sex has been cheapened to sell products in the market place, or worse — that it has been used as a weapon to create acts of violence between people. Sexually transmitted diseases are only one result of misused sexual energy.

There are psychological, social, economic, and moral crises that have developed, resulting in much human suffering. People must rebel against the commercialization and misuse of this sacred energy! The misuse has turned a force of unity and creativity into a vehicle for satisfying selfish desire and for causing human degradation and manipulation. The abuse of sex has divided people and made it an issue of law, of politics, and of the courts. Sex has become big business, increasing the wealth of manufacturers, pharmaceutical companies, doctors, lawyers, and entertainers, while adding a greater burden on society and hurting freedom.

For many, the search for sex and the demands of its consequences have replaced the search for the purpose of life. We must broaden our concept of sex and increase our different ways to express it. In all creative, constructive relationships, the energy of sex may be present on different levels, in different forms. Sex is energy exchanged between polarities in order to create something new. Many active and creative people use that energy in their work and are not preoccupied with satisfying the physical drive for sex.

❖

Sex can be an important part of a relationship only after the individuals have achieved a sense of responsibility toward each other, a sense of commitment and trust.

❖

We have been brainwashed into believing that love and intimacy in relationships can only be achieved through physical sex. Sex can be an important part of a relationship only after the individuals have achieved a sense of responsibility toward each other, a sense of commitment and trust. Sex should be a result of a creative, purposeful relationship on many levels.

❖

We have been programmed to have our sexual desire stimulated every time we see objects that have been associated with sex.

❖

We have let ourselves become brainwashed and manipulated by sex merchants because they appeal to a natural desire in us and in nature. However, in their advertising campaigns they have used sex to sell everything from toothpaste to automobiles. Every aspect and necessity of life has been made a symbol for sex by advertisers. The result is that in our society now are millions of objects and situations that are push-buttons to arouse our sexual desire. Even our clothing and hairstyle can release subconscious sexual images in people. No wonder that sexual abuse and misuse are epidemic. Compulsive shopping is another way these push-buttons activate us. We think that possessing the objects will satisfy our desires.

❖

It is ironic that we talk about sex as a freedom when most people are slaves to it!

❖

Much of our lives is controlled by sex. It is a major factor in the life style choices people make and it influences the self-image they create. It has even increased our taxes and has become an issue in national politics. Unwanted pregnancies have resulted in unwanted children and in abortions. These are burdening our society financially, socially, and psychologically. Many young people's dreams and purpose in life are cut short by an unwanted pregnancy. The Rev. Jesse Jackson once said, "There is no such thing as illegitimate children, only illegitimate parents. All children are children of God." This is true, but these "children of God" are becoming the nation's poor, the nation's abused, the nation's

❖ FRIENDSHIP, LOVE, MARRIAGE, SEX❖ 131

under educated. How can we waste the precious gifts of life? Misuse of sex is destroying human beings and the future of society in the process.

❖

It is stupid to talk about freedom of choice in our society when most people can't even choose to control their sexual desire.

❖

Now, many people cannot even enjoy sex without worrying about AIDS, in addition to other things. Because of the epidemic of AIDS, two people who love each other should voluntarily get tested for the HIV virus. Love is caring and feeling responsible for the welfare of the one you love. In love, each partner should want to do the utmost to help the other pursue his or her goals.

❖

In true love, we would never want to harm the one we love.

❖

The old line was, "If you love me you'll go to bed with me." The new line must be "If we love each other, we will get tested for HIV." While the old line was selfish pressure to force a partner into sex, the new line is a recognition of responsibility, trust, and protection of the one we love.

What is commonly called "sex" is just one way of expressing the life-giving, creative energy in the universe. If we broaden our definition to include other forms of relationship and creativity, new possibilities will open up. Emotionally, mentally, and spiritually we can create relationships, we can conceive great ideas, we can labor to give them birth for the benefit of humanity and the planet.

❖

The energy we call "sex" can be expressed in other ways to give life to our ideals and energy to our work.

❖

When we are devoted to a cause, an idea, or a goal, we use our sex energy as enthusiasm and drive. When we communicate with people and inspire them and draw inspiration from them, we feel creative and fulfilled. When love for a person, for an idea, or for a project makes us want to improve and work hard, we are using the life-giving energy creatively. Creative people, teachers, artists, people who serve others, organizers, many serious students, and others get tremendous energy by drawing their sexual energy up to emotional and mental levels.

Bodily desires are legitimate and must be satisfied in beautiful and harmless ways. However, we must not become slaves to them, or become selfishly obsessed by them. Like anything in nature, bodily desires must be dealt with appropriately and be under our control. People who use their sexual energy for creative expression on emotional, mental, or spiritual levels do not lust for sex because they are not focused on their *selfish* bodily desires and instincts. They are fulfilled and are feeling the power and energy of their inner creative force. Their sex has purpose, meaning, and creates beautiful relationships.

*Our focus in life determines
the quality of our relationships.*

When people are only focused on their body, they only satisfy their body during sex. When people are focused on their emotions, mind, and higher goals in life, they experience greater, more complete satisfaction during sex. Additionally, they are more complete human beings.

Our focus in life determines the quality of our relationships. If we are focused only on our body, we will make friends and partners who only want our body. If we are working for a great ideal, our friends will come from the ranks of our co-workers. They will love us for our dedication, for our thoughts, for our enthusiasm, for our inner beauty. We will develop real, lasting relationships that will help us reach our goals, and we will inspire others. We will experience a love that is not shallow, temporary, or selfish.

Long-lasting, eternal love is what we dream of in a relationship. We want to be loved for who we are. We want to trust our partner so we can give ourself to him or her, so that we both become more complete. We want a partner who will support us, inspire us, and encourage us to be all that we can be. We want our relationships of love to have the sincerity, discipline, and perseverance which are ingredients of any successful relationship or project.

❖

The standards of our friendships are formed from the standards of our life.

❖

We must not cheapen ourself, put ourself down, or lower our expectations for ourself. Even if we experience failures in our life and see our shortcomings, we should not lower our self-image. Our self-image is not what we are, but what we dream of becoming. Our dream for our future comes from our soul, urging us to go forward, to shape up, to strive for success. A cheap or failed relationship can drag us down, make us lose our path, destroy our self esteem, drain our magnetism. We must keep our standards high.

❖

If a "friend" wants us to lower our standards, he or she is not a friend.

❖

A true friend respects our integrity and values, and admires us for them. We will find our true love as we seek our true goals with integrity. We will find a partner in marriage, if that is what we need and want, who will help us on our path. We will make friends who will last a lifetime.

With integrity, our sex life will be purposeful and fulfilling. We will not be limited to the temporary pleasures of body, but will be fulfilled emotionally, mentally, and spiritually as well. Sex will become for us a creative force which we may express in our work, in our speech, and in our dedication to serve. The right use of sex energy will be like gasoline for our car to take us on important journeys of long duration. If we misuse sex, we will be putting our gasoline in a bottle, lighting it, and blowing ourselves up.

Sex is too important and too dangerous to misuse and abuse. It is not a recreational sport, it is not a fast-food place to satisfy our hunger, it is not a weapon to hurt others, it is not clothing to dress our ego, it is not a clinic to get over our hang-ups! People misuse sex to control others. We must not let ourselves be controlled, not by advertisers, not by movies, not by false friends, not by our own appetites.

❖

We must ask ourselves if we are ready to give a child all that its body and soul needs for a successful future.

❖

Sex has the potential to bring a living human being into this world. What a responsibility that is! We must ask ourselves if we are ready to give a child all that its body and soul needs for a successful future. Can we help a helpless soul, who depends on us, find its place in the jigsaw puzzle of life? So many unwanted children are trashed by careless, desperate, and unhappy parents, their lives and futures wasted. Heartless societies don't even throw these castaways a life-saving ring of hope. They become our shame and our burden.

❖

*Parenthood is the most important and creative job in society.
Nevertheless we get less training for it than we do to drive a car!*

❖

Good parents create a better future for society. They produce children who are healthy, have good values, have goals in life, and feel responsible for others and for nature. Ignorant or selfish parents produce children who will suffer, cause their parents and families to suffer, and be a burden to society.

❖

We need to demand of our leaders to raise the status of parenthood to that of other professions.

❖

Enlightened and successful parents must come together with teachers and with creative and successful people to design training for parents. Society must make training for parenthood a priority and easily available. The type of parent one is is a reflection of the type of human being one is. Therefore, the focus of training to be a parent should be on self-improvement, on human relations, and on developing creativity.

Imagine that a parent must conceive a healthy child, provide a healthy environment for its development for nine months, provide nurture, guidance, and education for another eighteen years, and then be there for advice, moral support, and love the rest of the child's life! A parent teaches a child all its most important lessons. A parent is a nurse, emergency medical technician, psychologist, spiritual leader, and economist. A parent can teach survival skills, practical skills, skills and interests to enrich leisure, human relations skills, and awareness of nature, society, and the universe. A parent teaches personal and social responsibility and citizenship. *For all these important tasks, no training is provided!* We expect people to become expert parents "on the job" without even a master parent to give help or guidance.

Most parents learn by trial and error or by just copying the examples of their own parents or of television parents. As a result, most parents feel desperate, stressed, worried, guilty, and helpless. They run to strangers who are "professionals" to help raise their children. Many parents, because they didn't have skilled parents themselves, raise their kids haphazardly or just let society raise them. What this means is that children are mostly "raised" by television and by their peers whose values are shaped by the media, by advertising, and by those who wish to manipulate and control the youth for their own selfish interests.

❖

There is no sense in having a child if parents and society are not prepared to give it the best guidance, the best environment, and the best opportunities for development.

❖

Only an informed and dedicated parent has the love and bond with a child to support its needs and protect its interests. A parent must therefore become a many-skilled expert. Parenting must be taken seriously as a top priority profession both by parents themselves and by society. Otherwise we are unrighteous to bring human beings to life. There is no sense in having a child if parents and society are not prepared to give it the best guidance, the best environment, and the best opportunities for development. We only increase the suffering of the world and the burden on the planet if we neglect children.

Many family budgets spend more on "toys" than on enriching and educational activities for their children. We cannot really blame them because they have been subject to advertising pressures and to images of a materialistic "good life" which they desired. Leaders in government have not set an example of advocacy for the basic needs of children either. For many years, budget priorities of government favored building strong weapons systems or enriching special interests more than investing in education, health care, and cultural opportunities for children.

People need to rebel against the priorities of the current pleasure-seeking and materialistic culture, and fight creatively for a better future for children. When the needs of children are met on the global scale so that all children may grow into successful adults, the causes of poverty, ignorance, unhappiness, and war will be eliminated.

❖

All people who care about the future should care about how they are affecting children.

❖

Young people need to realize that their whole youth is training for their most important job: being a mother or a father. Even if one does not personally have a child, the psychology and responsibility of motherhood and fatherhood must overshadow all of one's behaviors and work. All people who care about the future *should* care about how they are affecting children. We must ask ourselves, "Are my behavior and values providing a good model for children? Are my activities improving society and the environment?" What is good for children is also good for people in general. However, in order to emphasize the seriousness of living rightly, we need to use the children as the measure of our thoughts, emotions, and actions.

Thus, the standards for being a good friend, a good partner in love, and a good parent are the same. They are the basis for all right human relations. To repeat: *a true friend will always lift you up, never bring you down.* A friend is encouraging and looks out for your best interests. Friendship will create more unity, love, and progress in the world. Friendship helps people find their purpose in life.

❖

*We must be friends
to ourselves,
to our parents,
to our acquaintances,
partners,
and co-workers,
to our children,
to society,
and to the planet.*

❖

There is beautiful meaning and symbolism in marriage: taking vows of commitment, responsibility, love, and perseverance. Two lives come together to serve a greater purpose. Their hearts and souls are united. The individuals give themselves to each other. The exchange of golden rings symbolizes this: A ring is a symbol of infinity; the gold represents the golden virtues, the real Self. Marriage represents trust in the ability of people to selflessly cooperate for a better future.

❖

The meaning and ideals of marriage can be applied to anything to which we devote ourselves.

❖

We can be married to our ideals, to our goals, to our vision for the future. We can marry our higher Self. We can marry our work. We can marry society and nature. Marriage is the unification of ourself to the object of our devotion. *Whatever we are devoted to in life, we become.*

We must rebel against the selfish images of cheap sex, treacherous "friends," and unfaithful partners in marriage that pervade our culture. Our lives must be meaningful, not soap operas.

We must awaken to the fact that mass-media advertisers have been obsessing us with the importance of our body and of selfish excitement. They have made us devotees of false icons. They have created selfishness, vanities, fear, and jealousy as a way of worship. They have commercialized life, blinding us to its meaning, purpose, and true beauty. Through their images of man and woman they have over-stimulated sexual desire to a point where it is out of control and a real danger to a person's health and success.

❖

Friendship, marriage, sex, and parenthood must reflect our high values, our noble purposes, and the dignity of our self and of others.

❖

Friendship, marriage, sex, and parenthood are all fulfilling spiritual roles. They must reflect our high values, our noble purposes. Through these roles we must express our love, creativity, and sense of responsibility to ourselves and to society. All that we do must contribute to the common good and give others inspiration and hope for the future and faith in human nature.

Friendship, marriage, sex, and parenthood are not *purposes*, but they are *opportunities* for us to demonstrate the power of right human relations — respect, cooperation, responsibility — and to demonstrate the right use of energy through creativity and service. These potentially fulfilling relationships are means for us to be more complete and to prepare us for success and a greater role in society. They are foundations for our joy and progress in life, if approached with the seriousness and respect they deserve.

CHAPTER VIII

WHAT IS THE ROLE OF SACRIFICE IN OUR LIFE?

It is very interesting that if you look up the word "sacrifice" in the dictionary, almost all definitions are from a selfish point of view. Even in a religious sense, "sacrifice" means to give up something to gain favor from God. Behind all these meanings of sacrifice, there is the motive of gaining something for oneself.

This common, negative concept of sacrifice is based upon two ideas that are false from the spiritual viewpoint. First, that what we have *belongs* to us, and, second, that we should always *expect rewards* for what we do. The materialistic way of looking at the world makes life a market place. The values of the market are to get as much as you can for as little cost as possible, and only make a "sacrifice" if it is to your benefit.

How different is this psychology from the stories and tales of heroes who sacrifice even to the death out of devotion and courage with no expectation. Even fairy tales like *Cinderella* or *Beauty and the Beast* dramatize the sacrifice of the pure of heart. The heroines' attitudes show how a person can value helping others without complaining and without self-pity. Even where there is no recognition or reward for one's work, one can be giving. The fact that they become rich princesses is symbolic in a spiritual sense of the joy and glory of their nobility. It is not the motive of their sacrifice.

❖

Heroism is the expression of devotion to a high purpose and of dedication to a higher good.

❖

We love such heroic tales of sacrifice because we feel a sympathetic response from our soul. We feel happy after such stories and have greater optimism and faith in human nature. How different is that feeling from the disgust and pessimism we feel in films of violence and destruction in which people and property are "sacrificed" to satisfy selfish greed and cruel passions!

❖

The individual piece of the puzzle sacrifices its separate, selfish interest to be a part of the whole.

❖

Heroism is the expression of devotion to a high purpose and of dedication to a higher good. It is the result of realizing that everything is life. It is a result of realizing that we are all part of the great jigsaw puzzle of life. The individual piece of the puzzle sacrifices its separate, selfish interest to be a part of the whole. To be a part of the picture, to fulfill one's purpose is the essence of all true sacrifice from the spiritual viewpoint.

The result of materialistic sacrifice is a feeling of loss. This feeling stimulates other negative feelings and irritation such as bitterness, jealousy, self-pity, increased desire, hopelessness, sadness, remorse. Because of our possessiveness, we consume ourselves with the acid of negativity when we give up something, when we do more than someone else, when we are not appreciated, or when we are called upon to share.

❖

The result of spiritual sacrifice is the feeling that we have found something unexpectedly that we were searching for all of our life.

❖

The result of spiritual sacrifice is the feeling of joy, freedom, willpower. It is the feeling that we have found something unexpectedly that we were searching for all of our life. It is a sense of who we really are, our inner strength. It is feeling connected with all other creatures. It is feeling great love and compassion. It is a feeling that our heart has expanded and is charged with energy, that our mind is clear and sees the purpose of life, that our body is magnetic and ready for action!

❖

The old definition of sacrifice is to give up, while the spiritual definition is to radiate.

❖

In the spiritual sense, creativity is sacrifice. If we observe nature, we see how sacrifice is a cycle of birth, productivity, death, and regeneration. The cycles of nature are nourished by give-and-take in a balanced flow. In our body, the heart at the center of our circulatory system is an example of a give-and-take mechanism in us. If the heart does not give, it cannot receive. If it stops giving, our body dies. A plant grows, blooms in color and fragrance and then dies. Yet in its blooming, it was pollinated. In dying, its fruit and seed mature, and after the seed falls to the earth and is buried, a new plant is born. One plant produces many seeds and nourishes other kingdoms of life. That is the plant's sacrifice.

The old definition of sacrifice is *to give up*, while the spiritual definition is *to radiate*. When we let our light shine we are sacrificing. When we serve others we are sacrificing. When we conquer the habits and desires of our bodies we are sacrificing. These three sacrifices go together to create a free, heroic life, if, and this is the big IF, *if* they are done naturally, without forcing, and without expectation.

❖

Sacrifice throughout all of nature is the result of all things fulfilling their purpose.

❖

We have sunlight because the sun fulfills its purpose. We have honey because flowers and bees are working together fulfilling their purpose. Sacrifice is absent when something is prevented from fulfilling its purpose.

In human beings, the mechanisms which prevent the free expression of our purpose are habits, prejudices, and fears; desires which take us in wrong directions; the imposition and programming by society which tries to manipulate and exploit us; our own sense of separateness and selfishness. All of these make our radiation smaller. We are less giving because we lack the current of power of our own inner potential.

❖

Our beneficial influence upon others is our sacrifice.

❖

The degree we are able to radiate our inner potential is the degree of our sacrifice. Our beneficial influence upon others is our sacrifice. The result of sacrifice is abundance, generosity, and prosperity. Some people seek riches to put in sacks to hide from others. Radiant people are sources of riches for others. When we sacrifice, the jewels flow from us to enrich the world. Our touch, our words, our actions uplift people, set a positive example, inspire them. We work energetically. We become a productive tree of life with riches for ourselves and for others. People are attracted to our "delicious fruits." Abundance is not to be stashed away but to be shared.

❖

In the future, sacrifice will become the natural foundation of all human relations.

❖

In the past, the concept of sacrifice was applied only to heroes, to super-human beings. In the future, sacrifice will become the natural foundation of all human relations. It will be the spirit of how people act and work with their friends, in their families, in their communities, nations, and throughout the world. Sacrifice will be the essence of health and will also be utilized in healing. Sacrifice will enable people to understand the forces of nature and will increase mankind's appreciation of nature. The result of appreciation of nature will be a greater desire to care for it and to not violate its laws.

❖

Sacrifice will enable people to understand the forces of nature and will increase mankind's appreciation of nature.

❖

What sacrifice comes down to is love in action. This love is not selfish love, it is not desire. It is the unconditional, non-possessive love which comes from the awareness that all is life and that we are all united. If each person feels that he or she is united with all other beings, then all action will be giving. When all give, when all radiate their energy and talents, then we will all experience abundance.

❖

*Not only are people destroying themselves pursuing selfish pleasures,
but they are destroying others,
and they are destroying the environment.*

❖

Selfish desire has pushed humanity to the brink of self-destruction. Not only are people destroying themselves pursuing selfish pleasure, but they are destroying others and they are destroying the environment. People are selfish because they want more. Yet selfishness is never satisfied. Rather than *more*, selfish, indulgent people end up with *less* — materially, psychologically, and spiritually. They become poor in their relationships with others, they become poor of health, and their enjoyment of life decreases. The only increase they experience is an increase in their fears, anxieties, sense of isolation, aggressiveness, envy, and dissatisfaction. Their self-indulgence hurts others, kills their love, and makes them unlovable. Self-indulgence creates emptiness.

❖

*Sacrificial people are the
flowers of humanity.*

❖

Empty people cannot sacrifice. Sacrifice is natural overflowing of one's richness. People who are full often do not realize they are sacrificing. They can't help it because they are full — full of energy, light, love, goodwill, and creativity. Sacrificial people are the flowers of humanity. They enrich their environment. The more they sacrifice, the more they renew their energy and gain inspiration.

❖

*Our purpose in life is how we contribute
our unique talents,
experiences,
and viewpoints
to the betterment of the whole.*

❖

Sacrifice is the result of being in gear with the purpose of our life. We have seen that no individual exists in isolation unless he or she isolates him or herself. All beings exist in relationship to others. Our purpose in life is how we contribute our unique talents, experiences, and viewpoints to the betterment of the whole. When we know our purpose, we develop the sense of responsibility. In acting responsibly, we are sacrificing. Our sacrifice increases as we increase our capacity to serve, increase our influence, and increase our responsibilities. This progression of expanding purpose redefines "sacrifice" as a natural consequence and expression of our self-actualization. It is the essence of our spiritual nature, radiating its power and virtue.

❖

In contrast to the materialistic definition of "sacrifice" as suffering, spiritual sacrifice results in greater and greater joy!

❖

The birth of an individual is like a pebble falling into the ocean from space. It will be lost in that great ocean unless it develops relationships. When it hits that ocean, its influence is seen by little rings or wavelets moving outward from the center in expanding circles. These radiating circles go on until they go away, absorbed by the greatness of the ocean. The greater the pebble, the greater waves it will make and the greater relationships and influence it will make on the ocean.

These outward radiating circles symbolize our expanding awareness of the ocean. They symbolize our relationships, influences, and responsibilities. They represent our increasing sacrifice. As we grow, we should expand our awareness, our service, and our unity with the whole ocean. Sacrifice makes us greater and defines our existence. As we awaken to our purpose in life, we cast away our isolation. We find our true Self. In so doing, we cast away the mentality of selfishness, self-pity, and suffering. We cast away the materialistic definition of "sacrifice" and replace it with JOY!

❖

Once we are on the path of sacrifice, our health, beauty, and magnetism increase.

❖

The role of sacrifice is to help us find our true Self. Once we find our Self, we exist. Once we exist, we cease the futile chase after all the false symbols of status which wastes our time, energy, money, and take us on wrong paths away from our purpose. Once we know our Self, we gain status through our sacrifice — through our growing influence and responsibility. Once we are on the path of sacrifice, our health, beauty, and magnetism increase because we are radiating our god-like qualities — our divine nature.

PRACTICAL EXPRESSIONS OF SACRIFICE

When we express our purpose physically, emotionally, and mentally, we are sacrificing. Sacrifice is giving ourselves for a greater good. In order to give, we must be pure and we must not be attached to what we have or what we do. Sacrifice increases our health, joy, energy, and freedom.

From time to time, our newspapers give accounts of heroic deeds by average citizens. When asked why they rushed into a burning house to save a child, why they jumped into a swollen river to rescue a struggling victim, why they jeopardized their job to expose corruption in their work place, their response is often the same: "I don't know, I just had to do it. I didn't even think about it, I just did it. I couldn't live with myself if I didn't do something."

❖

The compulsion to do the right thing, and to selflessly meet the needs of others are dramatic ways of showing people that sacrifice is possible because of love, compassion, and the sense of responsibility.

❖

Every day we may sacrifice in many ways — even if they are not so dramatic or visible. Whenever we put ego, pride, and selfish interest aside we are making a sacrifice because we are coming closer to our true nature.

Physically we sacrifice when we use our body to fulfill our purpose, when we develop good habits of health, and discipline our body. Our body must be under the control of our intelligence, guided by the virtues of our heart so that it works in harmony with the best interests of ourself and others.

❖

How is self control a form of sacrifice?

❖

Our body wants to pursue its pleasures and rule our life with its hunger, sex drive, illnesses, laziness, or activity. When our body rules, we think it is the king. By elevating our forces of motivation to our true purpose, we "sacrifice" the drives of the body to discipline.

That part of our nature that lives for the pleasures of the body experiences "sacrifice."

❖

Frequently we meet temptations which test our ability to physically sacrifice.

❖

For example, we may be studying for an important exam the next day when some friends come by and invite us to share a six pack of beer and play some cards. Are we able to refuse for the sake of our exam? Can we make that physical sacrifice? Athletes experience physical sacrifice when they are in training and must discipline their bodies with proper diet, ample rest, and demanding training schedules.

❖

Emotionally we sacrifice when we love.

❖

Love is thinking of others before we think of ourself. If we analyze the source of most troubles, bad relations, and unhappiness, we will find a lack of love. When we don't love, we are selfish. We have self-pity, jealousy, hatred, and we desire to be accepted and to be loved. We experience extremes of excitement and depression. When we don't love, we become lonely and wrapped up in ourself. We would do almost anything to be loved.

When our emotions are not oriented toward giving but toward getting, they control our lives. Giving is sacrifice. When we give emotionally, we encourage others, we comfort others, we give hope. Emotional giving can heal others because it removes negativity from their system and replaces it with the joy of a loving heart.

❖

We know that people can improve if the good in them is encouraged and if we love them.

❖

There are three qualities of emotional sacrifice: love, forgiveness, and devotion. All of these represent the future orientation of sacrifice. When we forgive the past wrongs, we do so because we understand and have compassion for imperfection and human weakness. Nevertheless we know that people can improve if the good in them is encouraged and if we love them. When we become devoted to a future ideal, we "sacrifice" all the limitations of the past. Love, forgiveness, and devotion to the future are the ingredients for improving the lives of others.

In our society we punish people who do criminal behavior. Most of these people are hardened to punishment and it doesn't cause them to want to change. They expect to be punished; they even *want* to be punished. They have been kicked physically, emotionally, and mentally all their lives.

Our nation was shocked when we witnessed on video tape the beating of Rodney King by police officers in Los Angeles. Few, however, asked how it was that he arrived at that time and place in his life to receive that beating. Rodney King had already received many beatings emotionally throughout his life. No one gave him a vision, no one took time to nurture the good in him. The beating that people watched was not an event, but rather the dramatization and continuation of a beating he was receiving his whole life. How many other "criminals" are really the victims of continual social abuse by a society that does not love its citizens, nor give them vision and opportunity for a better future?

❖

Criminals are people who have not been loved, have not been forgiven, and have not been given a vision.

❖

Most people in our society will respond to love and forgiveness. More than anything else in the whole world these are what people want, and they are the main keys for turning one's life around. People who are loved start to learn how to love. They learn to love themselves and to love others. This love is the seed of the sense of responsibility. We often try to teach responsibility through rules and threats. These may produce certain controlled behaviors, however, they work on fear and upon the animal side of human nature. These methods do not produce the sense of responsibility which is inner authority and self-control.

❖

If one has no love, one is incapable of feeling responsible.

❖

Why is abuse — abuse of oneself and others — increasing in society? With all of our scientific, legalistic, and religious knowledge, rules, and spending, people continue to hurt themselves and others. This is because science, law, and religion are mainly controlled by materialists who use fear rather than love as their means of operating and influencing others.

There are many stories of abused and abusive people whose lives have been turned around when someone took an interest in them and loved them. Many teachers and counselors have had this effect on students. These success stories are the rewards that keep these professionals going.

The life and work of America's 1992 National Teacher of the Year, Thomas Fleming, is such a story. Himself a school drop-out and illiterate young adult, he recounts how the people who loved him, gave him a vision for the future, and encouraged him caused him to overcome the obstacles in his life. He earned a Master's degree and has devoted his life to helping young people who are abused, abusive, and heading for a dead-end, to turn their lives around. Many teachers have factual examples of the power of love to salvage young lives which are going in the wrong direction.

The fact that crime exists, that drug abuse exists, that child abuse exists, that spouse abuse exists, that sexual abuse exists, that there is homelessness, and an increase in physical and mental illness is evidence of a lack of love in our society. Even the pollution of our environment is an indication of an absence of love and devotion to an ideal for the future. The practical expression of emotional sacrifice is putting love in action to try to do whatever one can to eliminate the above social ills that have been created by selfishness and fear.

❖

How does one sacrifice mentally?

❖

Most people confuse the mind with the brain. However, the brain is not the mind, just as the computer is not the one who is using it. Mental sacrifice involves the development of the powers of thinking and understanding for the purposes of expressing one's soul and of serving man and nature.

❖

Most of what is commonly called "thinking" is just mechanical recall, conditioned by physical and emotional desires, or by programmed responses.

❖

The brain is a powerful sense organ and a highly sensitive computer. It records and stores a multitude of sensory impressions through its vast complex of neurological cir-

❖ THE ROLE OF SACRIFICE ❖ 159

cuitry. When people activate it by giving the right code or by pushing certain buttons, they can recall much information just like a computer. However, recalling information and even associating different information are not thinking; is not the mind. Most of what is commonly called "thinking" is just mechanical recall, conditioned by physical and emotional desires or by programmed responses.

❖

People live from day to day on automatic pilot, basically in a state of hypnosis.

❖

Most people do not really think. When a person says, "I changed my mind," it is usually because of conflicting desires, because of pressure from others, or because of an unconscious impression from his or her soul. People live from day to day on automatic pilot, basically in a state of hypnosis. They are living by habit, responding unthinkingly to cues. We already discussed in previous chapters how advertising and politics use this conditioning to control our tastes, motives, and opinions.

Even when we are in school increasing our knowledge, we are not really thinking. We may be accumulating knowledge, gaining skills, or learning new associations. We are learning valuable disciplines of organization and logic, but these are just the kindergarten of true thinking.

Our society values people with encyclopedic knowledge but most of this "knowledge" is used to deal with the material world and to fulfill basic needs, desires, or pride. This use of "the mind" does not bring fulfillment nor meets the serious needs of life or of the spirit.

❖

A person does not truly become an individual until he or she can think and act without automatically responding to pre-conditioning.

❖

The mind is the energy field by which we are able to contact the purpose of our soul and coordinate and discipline our physical body, our emotions, and our knowledge in order to serve the needs of society and of the planet. A person does not truly become an individual until he or she can think and act without automatically responding to pre-conditioning. The unconditioned mind thinks in the light of the highest virtues of the soul and produces action in harmony with the greatest good. A person does not truly become free until he or she can think without being controlled by physical or emotional desires, by prejudice, by fear, by anger, by public opinion or by traditional, political, or religious dogmas.

❖

A true thinker would never use knowledge to harm others because true thinkers know the consequences of what they are creating.

❖

Proof that knowledge is not a function of true thinking — of the mind — is the fact that it is frequently used for immoral purposes, or because it ignores the true needs of humanity. People must question how a riot caused by human despair can erupt just beyond the doors of a university, how crime and poverty can grow at the feet of the temples of government, and how drugs and sex can be pedaled in the halls of financial institutions! People must question why scientists have created the most horrible weapons of mass destruction, why we have industries which pollute our air and water, why many products necessary for the "good life" cause cancer, why so many millions are spent for unnecessary research while the basic needs of the world's children are neglected. People must question why the mass media are used to teach crime, prostitution, abusive relationships, and to promote ugly, horrifying, and disgusting images. A true thinker would never use knowledge to harm others because true thinkers know the consequences of what they are creating.

❖

Mental sacrifice is to use our energies for the fulfillment of the purpose of life and to create a better future for all.

❖

By now one should be able to realize that life has a purpose beyond the perpetuation of misery or the temporary satisfaction of desire.

"Purpose of life" is not abstract if we can develop our mind to penetrate into the treasure house of our soul. Our soul knows all, and knows what needs to be done for the benefit and improvement of self and society.

*When we sacrifice mentally,
we sacrifice selfishness,
prejudice, habits, and pride.
We are able to separate what is
real from what is false.*

We are able to discriminate true thought from the mechanical responses of our programming. We are able to live a life of self-control and purpose, in harmony with our conscience. Mental sacrifice expands our consciousness, lifts us out of the narrow hole of material selfishness, and makes us a responsible citizen of the universe. Mental sacrifice makes us creative and full of joy.

*The essence of the practical expression of
sacrifice is to find a need that we are
capable of meeting,
and then to act to meet it.*

When we do so, we must not encounter any resistance from our body, emotions, or mind. Neither must we act with expectation for reward. Our motivations must be to purely serve however we can. To sacrifice is to give up all impulses, habits, and behaviors which prevent us from expressing the qualities of our soul. It is the willingness to discipline ourselves so that we may improve and gain the necessary skills in order to help improve life for others.

❖

*To sacrifice is to give up all
impulses,
habits, and
behaviors
which prevent us from expressing the
qualities of our soul.*

❖

CHAPTER IX

HOW TO PREPARE FOR THE FUTURE

One afternoon on a canoe trip of several days and many miles, I came to a huge lake that had to be crossed in order to go back home by nightfall. I had just emerged from a side canyon formed by a tributary of this lake along the Colorado river. Leaving the protection of the steep red walls, I approached the open water. A strong wind blasted me in the face. Large wind waves buffeted me and I made hardly any forward progress. Ahead I saw a cove with low rocks. I made my way there and went ashore to assess my condition and rest. I ate, rearranged and tied down my gear, found a shady spot under a ledge of rock, and waited. After an hour and a half, the wind changed its direction slightly and the waves were not whipping as high. I decided to cross the lake to the other side and then proceed along the shelter of the opposite shore. I still had three hours of paddling even under the best of conditions.

Once my decision was made to go on, I had to continue without pause for rest. During hours of constant pushing against wind and water, the canoe progressed. Finally, as the sun began to set, the wind died to a breath of breeze.

As the first stars came out, I saw the grey-violet silhouette of my destination come into view on the other side of the lake. Each dip of the paddle caused the stars to dance in the blue-black mirror of the water. Exhausted, filled with the power of my accomplishment, and overwhelmed by the beauty of the night, I felt suspended on a trail of stars as my canoe cut a silver trail home.

❖

Our childhood and youth form a tributary leading to a great lake.

❖

The canoe trip above can symbolize the passage from childhood to adulthood. In youth we are protected to a degree by steep walls — we have limits which protect us. However, as we approach adulthood, we leave the protection behind and enter open waters where we are on our own. We must paddle our "canoe" to its destination, using skill, judgment, planning, courage, and determination. We must meet the challenges head-on but not be foolhardy. In the "open waters" of adulthood we gain experiences of success and failure as we make our way. How may we prepare ourselves for our journey to our destination?

❖

*In order to plan for the future we have to have some concept of our future —
we have to have a destination.*

❖

It is the magnet of the destination of home that motivates a person to continue his or her journey, even in the face of strong head winds and waves which cause delay, fear, or discouragement. Such threats test one's skill, judgment, and determination. To plan for the future is to challenge ourself with the vision of a goal or of a destination.

❖

A goal is the most powerful force for change and self-improvement.

❖

I had a student once who for two years had no self-discipline, no interest in school, and didn't care if she failed her classes. She came to school mainly to see her friends and just barely passed her classes.

The third year started out the same for a couple of months and then I noticed a change happening. She started paying attention, doing her work, and asking questions. She was organized, attentive, and started getting above-average grades. I wondered at her transformation. Talking to her I learned that she had started a vocational nursing program. She spent the afternoons in a convalescent home for old people, taking care of them as part of her study of nursing. She said she wanted to become a nurse.

Two years of begging, bribing, reasoning, and threatening did not change her motivation. Neither parents, teachers, principals, nor counselors could get her to shape up. It was only the goal of becoming a nurse that caused her to develop her potentials. It was the responsibility and caring for others that caused her to become responsible and care for herself. *These two things: having a goal and serving others are the keys to preparing for the future.*

❖

Goals shape our choices and are the main force of discipline in our lives.

❖

Setting goals is the first step in planning for the future. Goals shape our choices and are the main force of discipline in our lives. If we have the goal to buy something, we don't spend our money on other, trivial things. We work, we save, and we get our desires under our control.

❖

Goals set deadlines and motivate us to act more efficiently and not to waste time.

❖

We all have had the experience of having to do a term paper. When we first get the assignment, we often procrastinate, daydream in the library, and hop around like a toad. As the deadline approaches, we become more serious in our research, more organized; we spend longer hours working, and discipline ourselves until we finish the paper. The goal of a deadline exerts a pressure on us to work to our limits and beyond them if necessary.

❖

When we have a goal we begin to do what is necessary in order to achieve it.

❖

If its necessary to learn a skill, we make efforts to learn it. If it is necessary to get information, we go to the library to get books to inform ourselves. If it is necessary to have money, we start making efforts to earn and to save more. Whatever sacrifice or discipline is necessary to achieve our goal, we usually will do it.

❖

Many people's "goals" are desires or obsessions which are imposed upon them from the pressures of outside sources.

❖

We have already talked about these pressures: advertisements; peer pressure; expectations by parents, relatives, or friends; traditions; social pressures; self-image pressures, and so on.

❖

A true goal, however, can be distinguished from a false goal because of certain characteristics.

❖

A false goal generally

1. is materialistic
2. involves emotions such as jealousy, desire for status, and desire for revenge
3. is for short-term satisfaction
4. when achieved, does not make us truly happy or satisfied
5. is an imitation of some image or is a response to outside pressure
6. can make us go against our values, judgment, and true self-interest
7. may produce irritation and hurt our relationships with others
8. makes us waste our time, energy, and resources

A true goal

1. is future-oriented
2. has to do with helping us to achieve our purpose in life
3. leads to efforts of self-improvement
4. is beneficial to ourselves and to others
5. motivates us — gives us energy and inspiration
6. makes us happy and improves our relations with others
7. challenges us and brings out our inner resources and potential
8. makes us organize our priorities and make sacrifices

❖

*Once we have set goals which
prepare us for the future,
we must check them every so often to
make sure they are relevant to
changing circumstances and needs.*

❖

There are two factors which may cause us to want to modify our goals. The first factor consists of changes that take place in us or in our life due to working for our goal. The second factor consists of changing needs due to changing social, environmental, or technological conditions.

❖

*What you know is not as important as
your willingness to learn and
your ability to adapt to
changing trends and expectations.*

❖

In many secondary schools, there are programs with business or professional people in order to help young people prepare for the future. This "youth motivation task force" aims at motivating students to stay in school by giving them career goals, role models, and information about what is expected of them as members of the workforce. One point is frequently stressed, no matter what the profession. Most of the task force speakers emphasize that what you know is not as important as your willingness to learn and your ability to adapt to changing trends and expectations.

❖
*Success depends on
continuous efforts to learn.*
❖

From an educational viewpoint, then, it is more important to learn how to learn than to just accumulate knowledge. Knowledge can become quickly obsolete, but the qualities of character which you develop will last forever. That's why study habits are extremely important. The good habits that are developed in school may give you a head start in your career. Also, we must try to learn new things outside our areas of confidence and comfort.

❖
*We must take risks and
challenge ourselves.*
❖

In taking different kinds of classes, we will learn new viewpoints and different ways of looking at the world. Not only will we become more well-rounded in our knowledge, but we will also learn to work with people who have different life styles, expectations, and points of view. Developing organized study skills and curiosity, taking responsibility for our education, and exploring new fields will all contribute to making us adaptable, flexible, skilled, and confident individuals who are ready and willing to take chances.

❖
*The key here is not to become stuck in
old self-images, comfortable habits,*

*and limited expectations.
Be open to new possibilities!*

❖

As we work to reach our goal, we gain experiences, knowledge, and understanding which enlarge our perspective and which even change our self-image. When this occurs, we may want to change our goals or modify them to fit our new awareness. Sometimes you may take a class which reveals a totally unexpected talent or aptitude in your nature. Sometimes you might have a teacher who inspires and encourages you in a different direction. Sometimes a new class will stimulate new interests in you, or give you new skills which can change your life. Even after we have set goals we must remain open to new directions.

The pursuit of each goal is a road on which we will encounter people and experiences which will change us. As we change, we may modify our destination, sometimes even enlarging our expectations. As we experience success and learn from our failures, our identity will take shape and our future will come into focus. The key here is not to become stuck in old self-images, comfortable habits, and limited expectations. Be open to new possibilities!

❖

*Changing social, environmental,
or technological conditions can cause us to
change our goals.*

❖

Changing conditions present changing needs. A person oriented toward the improvement of self and society will always respond to the needs of others and of the planet. This is partly because of adaptability, but it is also due to selflessness, compassion, and sensitivity to the need. One can change one's goals without changing one's purpose in life. Different goals present different expressions of one's purpose.

An example of changing goals due to changing conditions occurred in 1974 during an oil embargo. A resource which had been abundant, cheap, and seemingly inexhaustible suddenly became scarce and expensive. Long lines formed at gas stations, and people could only purchase gas on certain days. Because of this crisis, people's values changed. No longer were large, powerful cars as attractive. Americans began to buy smaller economical ones. People began to adapt to changing environmental, social, and economic conditions. Automobile manufacturers had to adapt to changing needs and changing values. The goals changed, while the purpose of having transportation remained the same.

❖

Throughout history, changes take place which begin new eras of human experience.

❖

Such changes are often called revolutions, but they can be seen as adaptive responses to social, technological, and psychological evolution. For instance, the invention of movable type and the printing press was a major change in human history. For the first time, reading and writing became important for the general public. The ability to read greatly raised the self-esteem and expectations of people. New possibilities opened up. Human intelligence, responsibility, and creativity began to increase. Communication between people of news and new ideas spread. This single change in technology changed political structures, religion, science, and economy. Society changed as people gained new options for social mobility that were not based strictly upon birth and social class. People started to play a greater participatory role in society.

❖

We can experience such "revolutions" in our life not just by adapting to changes but by creating changes.

❖

To help ourselves adapt to rapid changes in society and in technology, we should try to develop the following useful qualities:

- self-motivation
- curiosity about the world
- a sense of responsibility
- flexibility and open-mindedness
- a devotion to broadening and sharpening our skills

These qualities will naturally increase our awareness, expectations, and self-esteem, and insure that our life is up-to-date and successful. However, the method *par excellence* for achieving psychological evolution and to touch the inner potentials of our spiritual nature is to use these qualities in a field of service to people or to nature.

❖

*When we challenge ourselves with service to others,
we create changes in our life which are revolutionary.*

❖

Service is to use our abilities to meet the needs of others. In service, the need we are serving becomes our main source of motivation. This replaces our usual preoccupation with and pursuit of selfish interests. Service opens our heart to others. Knowledge gives us the tools with which to act, but it is service which is action. Our gifts increase through sharing them. Through service we develop our understanding, our leadership, our abilities, and our sense of responsibility. We become more compassionate and more sincere in our relations with others.

❖

Service prepares us for the future because it is based upon a vision of the future.

❖

We serve because we want to help improve conditions. Any legitimate task or occupation can be a field of service. The difference between just doing your job and serving is that service is working with passion. When you serve, you are not working simply for personal reward but rather to fulfill an ideal of some kind. In service we feel satisfied because we experience the energy of our soul. Simply working out of a sense of duty often leaves us tired and desirous of escape. On the other hand, service often inspires us and gives us joy. When we serve to the point of fatigue, we are able to recharge ourselves with peaceful rest.

Service prepares us for the future, then, because it is based on a vision, because it increases our motivation and skills for improvement, and because it energizes us with the passion of our heart. These three elements are characteristics of a successful person and of a leader. As we set goals which are aimed at improving conditions and then serve goals loyally, we improve our own life. We become leaders of our own life rather than dry leaves blowing this way and that. We have direction, and because we have direction we are able to give direction to others.

Many people are bored and aimless. In such a state, they fall into the trap of living for selfish pleasures. They can be controlled by others and end up wasting their time, energy, money, and health. They never experience joy or the satisfaction of achieving their purpose in life.

True rebellion is to work for a great vision, to travel to a destination.

In rebellion with purpose, you rebel against all goals, attitudes, and expectations which limit the achievement of a future vision of improvement. You rebel against habits and narrow-mindedness, against manipulation and pressures which try to control you. You rebel against the forces of stagnation and degeneration which try to stop your progress on the path to perfection. You rebel against negativity, fear, and defeatist attitudes. You rebel against those who try to put down the human spirit, who try to cage it and clip its wings. A person who truly rebels becomes a pioneer and trailblazer seeking a promised land. Such a person is a source of hope, of health, and of enlightenment. Such a person lives a life which has meaning and purpose.

*Such a rebel serves humanity,
increasing light,
love, and
beauty in the world.*

GLOSSARY

ego: The personality when it is motivated by selfishness. When the person lives to satisfy the physical body, the emotions, or the mind, even if it hurts oneself or others. It is also referred to as the **false self**.

Inner Guide: The voice of our conscience — the qualities and standards of our most noble virtues. That which communicates our spiritual essence, our soul qualities, or our spiritual destiny to our mind, or warns us when we violate them.

path: Used to indicate the experiences and influences which shape a person's outlook, motivation, and knowledge about life. It is formed when one finds the purpose of one's life and uses all that he or she knows and *is* to work for that purpose. In such a case it is also referred to as the **spiritual path**.

self: (small "s") One's personality. The body, emotions, and mind usually shaped by environmental, social, or subconscious influences. Who one thinks one is. The mechanical person in contrast to the **true Self**.

Self, true Self, real Self: (large "S") The awakened or conscious individual who lives according to his or her soul qualities. The highest level of a person's development which is revealed as one progresses on the spiritual path.

soul: The individual's inner motivation. The uplifting energy coming from one's virtues or one's higher nature. That seed of potential in a person which blooms as one seeks to discover one's true purpose in life.

spirit: The energy in the universe which creates forms and life. Its qualities are intelligence, love, and will power.

spiritual: Progressively expanding toward the purpose of life. It is leaving behind gradually all the hindrances of the body, emotions, and mind.

SUGGESTED READING

There are many books available through SNS Press which expand upon the topics of self-improvement and self-realization. The following books are inspirational as well as informative for the serious student who wishes to further investigate and release his or her inner potential.

Bushell, Sylvia
Paths to Leadership: Power Through Feminine Dignity. This book is a beginning step for women to realize their potential powers of leadership and to use them in partnership with men to improve life.

Saraydarian, Torkom
The Purpose of Life. What is the purpose of life? How to find it; how to plan for it; how to practically work for it. Purpose as revealed in these pages is the essential factor in one's future.
The Flame of the Heart. This book is about the heart, about the core of our being. Many prob-

lems will be overcome as the heart is developed to balance the mind.

Dynamics of Success. An integrated approach on how to achieve success in whatever you want to do in life. The physical and material requirements as well as the spiritual qualities needed for everlasting success are examined.

The Hidden Glory of the Inner Man. The path of progress is nothing else but the process of knowing and becoming oneself. This book investigates the human soul and one's higher nature.

Sex, Family, and the Woman in Society. This book covers the whole range of topics from sexual relationships to building family unity, to women in jobs and in politics. A most comprehensive guide for the woman (and man) of the twenty-first century.

I Was. Dramatic reflections of a Hollywood star written in poetic verse as she evaluates the value and effect of her life on others. Her spiritual realizations give insight into the process of self-discovery, and into how to deal with failures caused by ego.

INDEX

A
abilities 22
abuse 14, 157
　of sex 128
abusive relationships 161
actions 112
activists 74
activities 85
adolescence 28
adulthood 92
advertisements 169
advertisers 135, 141
advertising 20, 21, 73, 80, 129, 138, 159
Africa 54
age 47
agriculture 60, 61
AIDS 131
alcohol 71
anger 34
animals 99
apathy 15
appreciation 46, 54
athletes 154
atoms 126
attachments 44
attitude(s) 37, 42, 70, 71
　toward life 31, 41

B
Bald Eagle 61
battle to improve life 10
being human 127
beauty 43, 63, 64
behavior 33, 37, 52, 53
　self-destructive 15
birth 151
bitterness 43
blind forces 101
bodily desires 132
boredom 26, 65
brain 158
budget 138

C
cancer 161
career 49
cause to work for 65
center of the universe 34
challenge(s) 88, 101 172, 176
　of teachers and students 9
　of youth 9
chance 24, 25
change(s) 108, 167, 175, 176
changing 173
child(ren) 135, 136, 137, 139, 161
　abuse 158
childhood 166
choice to fail 69
choices 37, 41, 43, 103
chores 64
classes 172
classroom 8
cliques 39
clone(s) 22, 57
colors 53
community 57
compassion 44, 63
competing goals 77
competition 34, 76
complexity 53
concept of life 51
conflict 15, 71
confusion 14, 15, 41, 43, 82, 84
conscience 106, 116, 189
consequences 160
conscience of a society 87
consumerism 81
contradictory goals 82
control 19, 35, 80, 85, 97, 111, 131, 132, 153, 168, 177
　of our life 30
controlling 107
cooperation 56, 58, 59, 78
cooperating for a common goal, 76
corruption 14
courage 20, 44, 63
creative forces 52
creativity 95, 96, 146
crime(s) 14, 63, 108, 158, 161
criminal behavior 155

criminals 156
crisis(es) 96, 107, 108, 109, 128
   created by success 108
cults 118
culture, destruction of 16

D
death 55
debt 79
dedication 49
defensiveness 15
deficits 16
degeneration 16, 66
dependence 70
desire(s) 20, 30, 33, 71, 74, 91, 97
   emotional 33
   mental 34
   which are controlling 31
depression 15, 55, 63
destination 30, 94, 167, 178
destiny 38, 102
destruction 37
dignity 46, 47, 142
direction 16, 42, 105
disagreement 58
disasters 76
discrimination 112
diseases 63
discipline 163, 168, 169
drives 32
drug abuse 158
drugs 63, 71, 161

E
economic crises 64
ego 33, 35, 70, 153, 179
electricity 126
emotions, uncontrolled 33
emptiness 34, 149
encouragement 48
encyclopedic knowledge 159
energy(ies) 52, 53, 56
   invisible 52
   of life 127
escapes 84
existence 90
expectations 169
exploitation 59, 66
   of others 34

F
fads 71
failing 72
Failing Is Not A Right 67
failure(s) 15, 44, 69, 70, 101, 134
   story of 15
fairy tales 89, 143
faith, religious 51

false
   friend 135
   friendships 121
   goal 167, 170
   images 84, 102
   life 71, 72
   teachers, 118
family 57
fate 24
fatherhood 139
fear 34
feelings 33
   holding on to negative 43
fighting back 114
Finding The Path 101
flatter 70
Fleming, Thomas 157
focus in life 133
forgiveness 44, 45, 155
form(s) 52, 53
   foundation of 148
frauds 118
free 42
"free" countries 77
"free" nations 75
freedom 16, 27, 43, 44, 50, 70, 72, 75, 76, 78, 80, 81, 83, 84, 85, 86, 88, 103
   from fear and pain 76
   of choice 131
friction 103
friend(s) 57, 71, 103, 121, 122, 134, 140
friendship(s) 113, 121, 122, 134, 140, 142
fulfillment 34, 62, 75, 76, 91, 96
future 8, 10, 30, 74, 101, 134, 139, 158, 165, 167, 177
   youth meeting challenges of 10

G
gifted 25
gifts 48, 91
give 91
   to others 31
give-and-take ecology 125
giving 34, 49, 56, 72, 91, 144, 149, 154
goal(s) 16, 23, 27, 31, 35, 44, 47, 71, 76, 77, 78, 79, 90, 167, 168, 169, 171, 173
   of life 32
God 52
good 48
gratitude 46, 48, 49
greed 34
growing up 27

guidance 116
guilt 15
gut feeling 110

H
habits 31, 32, 71, 102, 162, 172
handicapped 25
haphazard life 14
happiness 48, 49, 62, 81, 96, 97, 98
hate 56
hatred 34, 43
having a child 138
health 37, 52, 53, 57, 63
heart 23, 34, 86, 98, 146, 177
help 45
heroes 22, 65, 76, 83, 84, 102, 143, 148
heroic deeds 152
heroism 76, 83, 144
history 21, 45, 50, 75, 87, 174
HIV virus 131
home 167
homelessness 158
honesty 63
hope 8, 10, 48, 63
human
    being(s) 24, 76, 127
        role of 65
    independence 73
    rights 73
    spirit, potentials of 10
humanity 59, 78, 87, 149
hunger 59
    of our soul 84
hurt, being hurt in the past 43
hypnosis 159

I
idols 37
illegitimate children 130
illness 15, 55, 158
image(s) 22, 23, 33, 37, 87, 108, 124, 161
    false 15
improve life 66
improve the lives of others 61
improvement 56, 62, 86, 109
    of life 90
imitation 22, 65
independence 69, 78
individual 160
injustice 64
Inner Guide 116, 179
inner potentials 119
insecurity 33
insights 51
integrity 72, 103, 135
intentions 112
interdependence 54

interdependent world 72
invisible
    energies 52
    world 52
isolation 54, 62

J
Jackson, Rev. Jesse 130
jealousy 34, 56
jobs 47, 50
journey 167
joy 10, 34, 49, 48, 87
judgment 35

K
King, Rodney 155
knowing our purpose 85
knowledge 55, 160, 161, 172

L
lack of love 158
law of
    attraction 124, 126
    attraction and repulsion 112, 125
leader(s) 16, 82, 84, 86, 94, 96, 136, 138, 177
leadership 85, 87, 95, 96
liberation 119
life 22, 23, 24, 32, 33, 46, 51, 52, 53, 65, 125
    as a challenge 25
    definition of 51
    energy 34, 53, 62
    foundations of 52
    goal of 16
    is a great gift 66
    on our planet 59
    "packaged" 14
    protection of 60
    style 21, 91, 130
    taking charge of your 28
    transformation of 45
limits 25
Living The Good Life 89
living by habit 159
love 33, 34, 44, 48, 55, 56, 57, 58, 63, 65, 66, 125, 126, 131, 132, 133, 154, 156
    for others 46
    how to express 56
    in action 148
luck 24, 112

M
magnet 112
magnetism 56, 112, 125, 134
man 53

manipulation 34
marriage 123, 140, 141, 142
marketing 81
mass media 82, 161
materialism 90
materialists 94, 99
maturity 47
measure of success 96
media 16
memories, 43
merit 23, 25
mind 23, 34, 158, 159, 160, 161
misuse of sex 131
mixed messages create such
 confusion 82
molecules 56
money 59
moods 33
Mother Teresa 63
motherhood 139
motivation(s) 41, 162
motives 16, 159
move on 116
movement 53
movie stars 47, 71
movies 135

N
National Teacher of the Year 157
nations 59
nature 72, 92, 125, 146
 protection of 61
necessities of life 84
need(s) 32, 48, 50, 61, 116
 of others 34, 49
negativity 65
new direction 104, 107
nobility 20, 95, 96
noble values 64

O
obsessions 11, 16, 26, 32, 33, 68, 71, 94, 113, 132, 141, 169
obstacles 113
oil embargo 174
oneness 54, 55
opinions 159
opportunities 39, 112
optimism 11
others 34, 35, 48, 54, 62, 65, 176

P
parent(s) 15, 116, 136, 137, 140, 169
parenthood 136, 142
parenting 138
part of the whole 144
partner 133, 134, 140
past 31, 43, 44, 108

path 101
peace 44
peer pressure(s) 114, 169
personality 102
pesticides 60, 61
picture, the big
 finding and completing 17
 seeing 16
planet
 life on our 55
plant 146
pleasure(s) 97, 153, 177
potential 99
pollution 14, 16, 59, 63, 64, 158
positive attitude 24
possessions 23, 33, 34, 91, 98
poverty 59, 161
power 22, 34, 44
 to think 23
pre-conditioning 160
prejudice(s) 39, 102, 162
pressures 169
pride 162
problems 63, 77
programming 29, 31
progress 44
prostitution 161
protecting people and nature 61
protection 114
pseudo-rebellion 65
psyche 52
psychic energy 52
purity 63
purpose 21, 23, 29, 31, 55, 69, 79, 80, 84, 103, 115, 122, 147
 for living 79
 of life 64, 93, 161, 162
 in life, 11, 38, 42, 50, 75, 84, 111, 119, 150, 174, 177
push buttons 29
puzzle(s) 13, 21, 53, 116, 127, 144
 finding one's place in the 13
 not knowing the picture of
  the 14
 of life 38, 46, 135, 144
 piece(s) 122
  people as 13
 story of trying to fit in
  wrong place in 15

Q
questions 51

R
racism 59
reality 90
reason for living 75

rebel 141
rebellion 74, 88, 178
    with purpose 178
recognition 34
relationship(s) 33, 54, 97, 98, 106, 113, 124, 125, 133, 151
    of love 134
resentment 43, 44
responsibility(ies) 42, 47, 48, 57, 66
revolutions 174, 175
respect 47, 48, 49, 50, 54
right choices 79
ring 140
riot 161
risks 172
role model(s) 22, 31, 35, 37, 70

S

sacrifice 143, 144, 145, 146, 147, 148, 150, 151, 152, 153, 154, 155, 158, 161, 162
    practical expressions of 152
satisfaction 34, 97
school(s) 8, 57, 82, 159, 171
    of life 115
science 51
scientists 161
search for sex 128
Self 19
    false 19, 31
        how built 19
    higher, 141
    real 179
    struggle of 19
    true 31, 50, 99, 102, 151, 152
self-centeredness 34, 55
self-control 156, 162
self-deception 70, 71
self-destruction 149
self-esteem 90
self-image(s) 15, 20, 22, 70, 80, 134, 172
self-improvement 62, 167
self-indulgence 149
self-motivation 175
self-pity 34
selfish desire 149
selfishness 33, 162
sense of
    gratitude 46
    proportion 24
    purpose 119
    respect 46, 47
    responsibility 24, 46, 48, 54, 78, 96, 156
    value 35
sensitivity 53

service 176, 177
serving 56, 119
sex 128, 129, 130, 131, 132, 135, 142, 161
    life 135
    merchants 129
sexual
    abuse 158
    desire 131
    energy 127
    sublimation of 132
sexually transmitted diseases 128
shortcomings 134
Sioux Indians 54
skill(s) 23, 169
slave(s) 35, 81, 87, 132
society 9, 47, 63, 66, 68, 74, 80, 81, 82, 87, 89, 131, 136, 155, 156, 159, 175
    regeneration of 10
    solving problems of 10
soul 112, 162, 180
    mate 124
    qualities 102
    starving 84
space 53
spirit 52, 180
    human 50
    within our heart 86
spiritual, 180
    activity 119
    direction 35
    life 119, 120
    nature 35
    path 101, 113, 114, 115, 120, 179
    teachers 117
spouse abuse 158
standards 134
stars 55
stereotyping 39
struggle 89
struggles of the human spirit 89
student becomes the text and teacher 11
students 12, 39
study
    habits 172
    skills 172
success(es) 16, 48, 62, 72, 87, 97, 101, 172
suffering 16, 58
sun 55
superiority 34
symbols 31, 38
symphony 53

T

talents 15, 16
tastes 159
tattoos 67
teacher(s) 9, 11, 116, 117
teaching
   is a privilege 7
   teenagers 7
team 58, 60
teamwork 59
technology 175
teenage mothers 103
teenagers 8, 65
temptations 154
term paper 168
test 96
thinker 160
thinking 24, 59, 158, 159, 161
thought 162
toys 138
tragedy 50
training 139
   for parenthood 137
transform 45
traps 20, 31, 88, 119
treasures 48
true goal 170
True Love 123, 131
trust 133, 141

U

ugliness 63
ugly motives 64
understanding heart 24
unemployment 59
United Nations 59
unity 45, 46, 57, 58
universe 53
   cooperation in 56
   does other life exist in 51
   knowledge of 51
university 161
unseen dimension of life 51
unwanted children 135

V

value(s) 16, 21, 22, 37, 42, 47, 63, 65, 70, 71, 72, 96, 142
   false 19
      effect of imposition of 19
   of life 64
   system 37, 41
vanity 20
vices 20
video game
   life as a 26
virtue(s) 20, 63, 74, 90, 102, 109, 116, 189

visible world 52
vision 10, 73, 74, 75, 109, 178
   nation without 17
   one's 17
   of the future 43

W

war(s) 59, 76, 77
waste 14, 46
wasting 177
   our resources 84
watchfulness 112
water 61
we reap whatever we sow 112
weapons of mass destruction 161
web of life 60, 69
willingness to learn 171
wisdom 55
work 46, 49, 85, 132
   for beauty 64
working to pay off the credit card 79
wrong choices 79

Y

youth 10, 87, 139, 166
   as a "problem" or a "market" 11
   as a "problem" 10
   motivation task force 171

ABOUT THE AUTHOR

Richard Sidy graduated from UCLA in 1968 with a BA in political science, specializing in political theory. He was active in community service projects including the Tutorial Project, the Experimental College, and Project Amigos, for which he worked in the barrios of Tijuana each school break. In the Spring of 1968 he took leave from his studies to work with the Poor Peoples' Campaign in Washington D.C.

After graduating, Sidy entered the Peace Corps in which he served for two and a half years in rural development in the West African nation of the Côte d'Ivoire.

Upon his return, Sidy earned his teaching credential in secondary education at UCLA. He taught Social Studies, Spanish and French for the Los Angeles Unified School District in south central Los Angeles, and in 1977 was selected to be on the founding faculty of their first magnet school, the Center for Enriched Studies.

In 1982 Sidy founded an innovative elementary school in Sedona, Arizona, emphasizing global education, environmental studies, science, and art in an integrated curriculum.

Currently, Sidy is a foreign language teacher with the Flagstaff Unified School District. Since relocating to Arizona, Sidy has helped organize and supervise student cultural exchanges with France, the Côte d'Ivoire, and with the Navajo, Hopi, and Zuñi people.

Sidy earned his Master of Education degree at Northern Arizona University in secondary education, focusing upon international education, multi-cultural education, and foreign language.

OTHER WORKS BY THE AUTHOR

WORLD DIPLOMACY

This book emphasizes that the choices and relationships made by individuals and governments in the next few years will decide how humankind will be able to live on this planet beyond the twentieth century. It provides guidelines for the transformation of individual relationships and international politics to eliminate needless suffering.

Price $8.95, 176 pages, softbound, ISBN: 0-9633744-0

EXPLORE U.S.A

Offering a hands-on, inquiry-based, integrated approach to U.S. history and geography, these reproducible activity and project cards are designed to be used by individual students, small groups, or whole classes. A 24-page teacher's guide provides presentation suggestions. Grades 4-8.

Price $19.50, 45 reproducible activity cards and guide

NEXT RELEASE:

SCIENCE, RELIGION, AND THE SEARCH FOR GOD
Bridging the Gap

In essence, science and religion are both seeking the same goal: to enable people to live a better life and to better understand their relation to others and to the universe.

This book explores the common ground of science and religion, providing options which reconcile their differences and prevent their misuse. When these two powerful forces in society join together, human culture and civilization may take the next step in its psychological and social evolution. Working together, science and religion may enable people to realize their purpose in life and dedicate themselves to a life of service in the light of spiritual understanding.

ISBN: 0-9633744-2-7

❖

SNS
PRESS

Foundations of Unity

> The books of SNS Press are dedicated to presenting new perspectives in intellectual and philosophical thought on a variety of issues of importance as humanity enters the twenty-first century. The ideal of unity is the thread which ties all these books together. Mankind now realizes, more than ever before, the necessity to create models of unity as goals for a better future.

Write to SNS Press to request a catalogue of the books mentioned in Suggested Reading, Other Works, and of other titles. You may order books directly from SNS Press or from your local bookstore.

If you have any questions or comments for the authors or wish to have them conduct a workshop or address your group or organization, please feel free to contact us.

SNS Press
380 Rain Tree Road
Sedona, Arizona 86336
United States of America

FAX (602) 284-9055